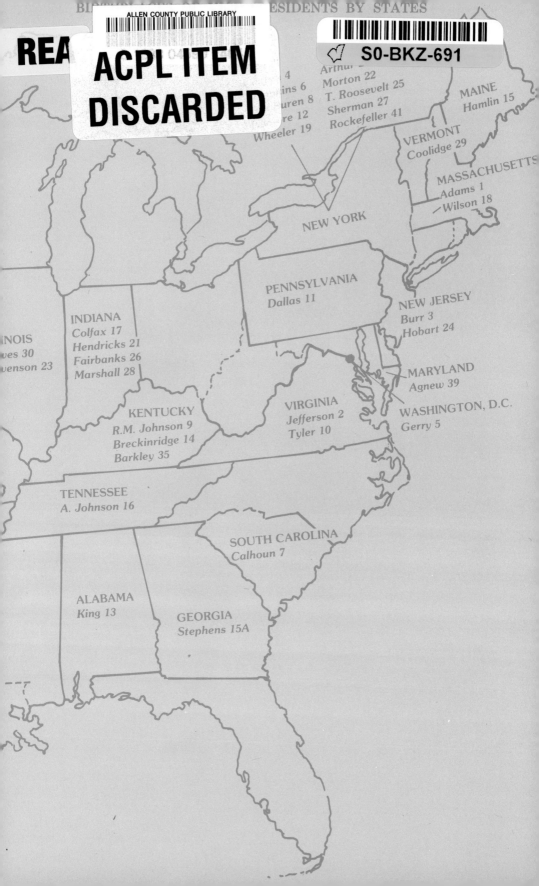

ALLEN COUNTY PUBLIC LIBRARY

ACPL ITEM DISCARDED

SO-BKZ-691

BIRTH... ...SIDENTS BY STATES

REA

4
...ins 6
...uren 8
...re 12
Wheeler 19

Arthur ...
Morton 22
T. Roosevelt 25
Sherman 27
Rockefeller 41

MAINE
Hamlin 15

VERMONT
Coolidge 29

MASSACHUSETTS
Adams 1
Wilson 18

NEW YORK

PENNSYLVANIA
Dallas 11

NEW JERSEY
Burr 3
Hobart 24

INDIANA
Colfax 17
Hendricks 21
Fairbanks 26
Marshall 28

...NOIS
...ves 30
...venson 23

MARYLAND
Agnew 39

KENTUCKY
R.M. Johnson 9
Breckinridge 14
Barkley 35

VIRGINIA
Jefferson 2
Tyler 10

WASHINGTON, D.C.
Gerry 5

TENNESSEE
A. Johnson 16

SOUTH CAROLINA
Calhoun 7

ALABAMA
King 13

GEORGIA
Stephens 15A

7-16-80

THE NEAR GREAT — CHRONICLE
OF THE VICE PRESIDENTS

A COLLECTION OF PHOTOGRAPHS AND INSCRIPTIONS
AND A RECORD OF HISTORICAL EVENTS

THE NEAR GREAT —
CHRONICLE OF THE VICE PRESIDENTS

By

ARCHIBALD LAIRD, Brig. General

*Author of MONUMENTS MARKING
THE GRAVES OF THE PRESIDENTS*

Photographs by Ruth Washburn Laird

THE CHRISTOPHER PUBLISHING HOUSE
NORTH QUINCY, MASSACHUSETTS
02171

COPYRIGHT © 1980

BY ARCHIBALD LAIRD

Library of Congress Catalog Card Number 79-53716

ISBN: 0–8158–0381–8

First Edition

(All Rights Reserved)

PRINTED IN

THE UNITED STATES OF AMERICA

THIS BOOK IS LOVINGLY
DEDICATED
TO MY WIFE
RUTH WASHBURN LAIRD

2112794

FAME

"Their noonday never knows
What names immortal are:
'Tis night alone that shows
How star surpasseth star."

John Banister Tabb

AUTHOR'S NOTE

The comprehensive nature of this book was made possible with the help and unselfish cooperation of dedicated librarians and persons interested in history. The only way the author can properly express his profound gratitude is by listing the individuals who provided essential information (either by letter or by personal interview) and those who supplied difficult-to-get pictures.

The books and other references consulted are included (and listed chronologically) in order to present the Vice Presidents in their proper perspective.

During the lustrum the author was gathering information, there was one indispensable person at his side: Ruth Washburn Laird. She was wife, chauffeur, photographer, and constant companion. Never tiring, she traversed thousands of miles in twenty different states and the District of Columbia, visiting hundreds of libraries, cemeteries, and historic places. Her words of encouragement were: ''Don't worry — we'll get there and we'll find it.'' All the photographs not specifically credited to others are hers.

When adverse weather and a long journey were about to delay the acquisition of some important facts, my son, Archibald Laird II, cheerfully volunteered to go to Bangor, Maine and visit the Mt. Hope Cemetery. His diagram of the Hamlin burial plot completed the basic project.

PICTURE CREDITS

Art Commission of the City of New York
Barrile, Valerie Francis, Buffalo Rotary Club, Buffalo, NY
Carter, Patricia Lee, Georgia Department of Natural Resources, Atlanta, GA
DeLucia, Vic, *New York Post,* New York, NY
Evanston Historical Society, Evanston, IL
Frazier, Tim, Staff Photographer, Tennessee Department of Conservation, Nashville, TN
Habernig, George, Kingston, NY
Habey, Ed, Uvalde, TX
Handley, Robert E., Evergreen Memorial Cemetery, Bloomington, IL
Kehoe, Barbara B., Evanston Historical Society, Evanston, IL
Kentucky Historical Society, Frankfort, KY
Laird, Ruth W., Wellsboro, PA
Library of Congress, Photoduplication Service, Washington, DC
Livitsanos, G. K., Livitsanos Photography, Totowa Boro, NJ
Logan, Becket, East 10th Street, New York, NY
Monaghan, Joanne, Bangor Historical Society, Bangor, ME
Niezgodski, Robert C., Old City Cemetery, South Bend, IN
Phillips, Helen M., Pioneer Hi-Bred International, Des Moines, IA
Preston, Douglas M., Oneida Historical Society, Utica, NY
Robideau, N., Robideau Studios, Malone, NY
Sanchez, Maria C., Topeka Cemetery, Topeka, KS
Tennessee Conservation Department, Nashville, TN
Tyler, Emily, Sherwood Forest, Charles City County, VA
Wachs, Robert F., Lexington Cemetery, Lexington, KY
Wright, Michael, Northern Indiana Historical Society, South Bend, IN

AUTHOR'S PREFACE

Shortly after *Monuments Marking the Graves of the Presidents* was published, many readers asked when a companion volume would appear on the Vice Presidents. While I had previously given little thought to the Vice Presidents, I was gradually influenced by such flattering suggestions. I was further prompted by the uncomplimentary comments found in many publications on those first in the succession line for the Presidency. Thus, I made a resolve to do for the Vice Presidents what had been done for the Presidents. For good measure, a summary of their achievements was added.

There is much truth in the statement once made at a nominating convention: "A man who is not big enough to be President is not big enough to be Vice President." A closer look at our Vice Presidents by way of the chronologies in this book indicates that they were, and are, important public figures and leaders in many fields of activity.

While the limitations of duties in the office of Vice President suggest that the holder is relegated to obscurity, it is important to know that the men who have served in the office had the superior qualifications needed to administer government at the Federal level.

A review of their lives shows that they rose to eminence in business, in the professions, in military and civic leadership, in personal and political magnetism, in philanthropy, and in administration before they were selected to fill the second highest office in the Republic. Those who were called when an emergency occurred were more than equal to the problem they faced. A glance at their records of achievement makes it evident that selection was based on a firm foundation of character, reputation, industry, sincerity, courage, patriotism, piety, sagacity, and practical common sense.

A visit to their last resting places reveals that they wrote their names high in the history of the Nation they profoundly loved and so loyally served; without exception, each is an inspiration to be remembered. Overshadowing the beauty and peacefulness that surrounds the graves are the historical connotations on the monuments.

Some monuments are artistically fascinating, others are arresting examples of the sculptor's art. All are immortalized by the legend on or near the last resting place. When just the name and dates appear, posterity visits libraries and archives to find out what the individual had done. Truly, these monuments are the history of the United States in stone.

The purpose of this book is evocative — to bring back into national memory the men who were eclipsed because of the title of the office they held. The book will also provide a way of preserving the inscriptions on the monuments, on which time and the elements are taking inexorable toll. It provides an accurate, comprehensive guide to the final resting places of outstanding statesmen. It records their accomplishments.

Archibald Laird

CONTENTS

ILLUSTRATIONS

CHRONOLOGY

John Adams (39)

Thomas Jefferson (45)

Aaron Burr (51)

George Clinton (57)

Elbridge Gerry (65)

Daniel D. Tompkins (71)

John Caldwell Calhoun (79)

Martin Van Buren (87)

Richard Mentor Johnson (93)

John Tyler (103)

George Mifflin Dallas (109)

Millard Fillmore (115)

William Rufus de Vane King (123)

John Cabell Breckinridge (129)

Hannibal Hamlin (141)

Alexander Hamilton Stephens (149)

Andrew Johnson (163)

Schuyler Colfax (171)

Henry Wilson (179)

William Almon Wheeler (191)

Chester Alan Arthur (199)

Thomas Andrews Hendricks (205)

Levi Parsons Morton (211)

Adlai Ewing Stevenson (223)

Garret Augustus Hobart (231)

Theodore Roosevelt (237)

Charles Warren Fairbanks (243)

James Schoolcraft Sherman (249)

Thomas Riley Marshall (259)

Calvin Coolidge (265)

Charles Gates Dawes (273)

Charles Curtis (281)

John Nance Garner (287)

Henry Agard Wallace (293)

Harry S. Truman (299)

Alben William Barkely (307)

Richard Milhous Nixon (315)

Lyndon Baines Johnson (321)

Hubert Horatio Humphrey (327)

Spiro Theodore Agnew (333)

Gerald Rudolph Ford (337)

Nelson Aldrich Rockefeller (343)

Walter Frederick Mondale (349)

DIRECTORY OF CEMETERIES

1	John Adams	Unitarian Church, Hancock Street, Quincy, MA.
2	Thomas Jefferson	Monticello, Charlottesville, VA
3	Aaron Burr	Princeton Cemetery, Wiggins at Witherspoon, Princeton, NJ
4	George Clinton	Old Dutch Church Cemetery, Main & Wall, Kingston, NY
5	Elbridge Gerry	Congressional Cemetery, E St., S.E. at 17th, Washington, DC
6	Daniel D. Tompkins	St. Mark's Church-in-the-Bowery, 10th St. at 2nd Ave., New York, NY
7	John Caldwell Calhoun	St. Philip's Church Cemetery, 146 Church, Charleston, SC
8	Martin Van Buren	Kinderhook Cemetery, Kinderhook, NY
9	Richard Mentor Johnson	Frankfort Cemetery, Frankfort, KY
10	John Tyler	Hollywood Cemetery, Richmond, VA
11	George Mifflin Dallas	St. Peter's Church Cemetery, 3rd & Pine, Philadelphia, PA
12	Millard Fillmore	Forest Lawn Cemetery, Delaware at Delavan, Buffalo, NY
13	William Rufus de Vane King	(Mausoleum) Live Oak Cemetery, Selma, AL

14	John Cabell Breckinridge	Lexington Cemetery, 833 W. Main St., Lexington, KY
15	Hannibal Hamlin	Mount Hope Cemetery, State St., Bangor, ME
15	*Alexander Hamilton Stephens*	Liberty Hall, Crawfordville, GA
16	Andrew Johnson	Andrew Johnson National Cemetery, Monument Ave., Greeneville, TN
17	Schuyler Colfax	Old City Cemetery, 214 Elm St., South Bend, IN
18	Henry Wilson	Old Dell Park Cemetery, Natick, MA
19	William Almon Wheeler	Morningside Cemetery, Malone, NY
20	Chester Alan Arthur	Albany Rural Cemetery, Menands-Watervliet, NY
21	Thomas Andrews Hendricks	Crown Hill Cemetery, W. 38th St., Indianapolis, IN
22	Levi Parsons Morton	Rhinebeck Cemetery, U.S. Rte. 9 S., Rhinebeck, NY
23	Adlai Ewing Stevenson	Evergreen Memorial Cemetery, 302 E. Miller St., Bloomington, IL
24	Garret Augustus Hobart	(Mausoleum) Cedar Lawn Cemetery, McLean Blvd. at Crooks Ave., Paterson, NJ
25	Theodore Roosevelt	Youngs Memorial Cemetery, Oyster Bay, L.I., NY
26	Charles Warren Fairbanks	Crown Hill Cemetery, 34th & Blvd. Place, Indianapolis, IN
27	James Schoolcraft Sherman	(Mausoleum) Forest Hill Cemetery, Oneida St., Utica, NY

28	Thomas Riley Marshall	(Mausoleum) Crown Hill Cemetery, W. 38th St., Indianapolis, IN
29	Calvin Coolidge	Village Cemetery, Plymouth Notch, VT
30	Charles Gates Dawes	(Mausoleum) Rosehill Cemetery, 5800 Ravenswood Ave., Chicago, IL
31	Charles Curtis	Topeka Cemetery, 1601 E. 10th St., Topeka, KS
32	John Nance Garner	Uvalde Cemetery, Uvalde, TX
33	Henry Agard Wallace	Glendale Cemetery, 4909 University Ave., Des Moines, IA
34	Harry S. Truman	Courtyard, Harry S. Truman Library, Independence, MO
35	Alben William Barkley	Mt. Kenton Cemetery, Lone Oak Rd., Paducah, KY
37	Lyndon Baines Johnson	Johnson Family Cemetery, LBJ Ranch, Johnson City, TX
38	Hubert Horatio Humphrey	Lakewood Cemetery, 3600 Hennepin Ave., Minneapolis, MN
41	Nelson Aldrich Rockefeller	Rockefeller Estate, Pocantico Hills, N. Tarrytown, NY

A LIST OF SOURCES

BOOKS ON THE VICE PRESIDENTS

1788   Gerry, Elbridge   *Observations on the New Consti-tution*

1828   Austin, James Trecothick   *The Life and Times of Elbridge Gerry*

1834   Emmons, William   *Biography of Colonel Richard M. Johnson*

1843   Van Pelt, Peter J.   *An Oration*

1851   Jenkins, John S.   *Lives of the Governors of the State of New York*

1872   Mann, Jonathan B.   *The Life of Henry Wilson*

1886   Holcombe, John W., and Skinner, Hubert M. *Life and Services of Thomas Andrews Hendricks*

1899   Hamlin, Charles Eugene   *Life and Times of Hannibal Hamlin*

1904   Smith, William Henry   *Life and Speeches of Charles Warren Fairbanks*

1908   Ridgely, Helen W.   *Historic Graves of Maryland and the District of Columbia*

1909   Hamlin, Myra Sawyer   *Eleazer Hamlin and His Descendents*

1910   Magie, David   *Life of Garret Augustus Hobart — 24th Vice President of the US*

1925   Marshall, Thomas Riley   *Recollections of Thomas R. Marshall, A Hoosier Salad*

1929   Winston, Robert W.   *Andrew Johnson, Plebian and Patriot*

1930   McElroy, Robert   *Levi P. Morton*

1932   Meyer, Leland Winfield   *Life and Times of Col. Richard M. Johnson*

1934   Hatch, Louis Clinton   *History of the Vice Presidency*

1939   Thomas, Charles M.   *Thomas Riley Marshall — Hoosier Statesman*

1943   Wallace, Henry A.   *The Century of the Common Man*

1944   Mackay, William Andrew, and Canfield, A. A.   *Murals in the Theodore Roosevelt Memorial Hall*

1948   Timmons, Bascom N.   *Garner of Texas*

1948   Young, Klyde, and Middleton, Lamar   *Heirs Apparent — Vice Presidents of the US*

1952   Smith, Willard H.   *Schuyler Colfax — The Changing Fortunes of a Political Idol*

1953   Timmons, Bascom N.   *Portrait of an American — Charles G. Dawes*

1957   Davis, Kenneth S.   *The Politics of Honor, A Biography of Adlai E. Stevenson*

1958   Barkley, Jane R.   *I Married the Veep*

1959   Rayback, Robert J.   *Millard Fillmore*

1959   Mazo, Earl   *Richard Nixon — A Political and Personal Portrait*

1959   Dietz, August   *Presidents of the United States of America*

1960   Kornitzer, Bela   *The Real Nixon*

1963   Merk, Frederick, and Merk, Lois Bannister   *Manifest Destiny and Mission in United States History — Millard Fillmore*

1964   Panofsky, Erwin   *Tomb Sculpture*

1964   MacArthur, Douglas   *Reminiscences*

1964   Spaulding, Ernest Wilder   *His Excellency George Clinton*

1965   Morison, Samuel Eliot   *Oxford History of the American People*

1965   Griffith, Winthrop   *Humphrey: A Candid Biography*

1966   Harwood, Michael   *In the Shadow of the Presidents — American Succession System*

1968   Wiltse, Charles M.   *John C. Breckinridge*
1968   Mazo, Earl, and Hess, Stephen   *Nixon — A Political Portrait*
1968   Dorman, Michael   *The Second Man*
1968   White, Norval, and Willensky, Elliot   *American Institute of Architects Guide to New York City*
1968   Irwin, Ray W.   *Daniel D. Tompkins*
1969   Seiverling, Richard F.   *Lewis B. Hershey — Pictorial and Documentary Biography*
1971   McKay, Ernest   *Henry Wilson: Practical Radical*
1972   Albright, Joseph   *What Makes Spiro Run — Life and Times of Spiro Agnew*
1972   Abbott, Richard H.   *Cobbler in Congress — The Life of Henry Wilson   1812–1875*
1972   Miller, Lillian B., et al.   *If Elected — Unsuccessful Candidates for the Presidency 1796–1968*
1973   Thompson, Davis S.   *HST — A Pictorial Biography*
1974   Burchard, John Ely, et al.   *Treasures of America*
1974   Miller, Merle   *Plain Speaking, Oral Biography of HST*
1974   Vestal, Bud   *Jerry Ford — Up Close*
1974   Davis, William C.   *Breckinridge — Statesman, Soldier Symbol*
1974   Barzman, Sol   *Madmen and Geniuses: The Vice Presidents of the United States*
1975   Kramer, Michael, and Roberts, Sam   *I Never Wanted to be Vice-President of Anything! An Investigative Biography of Nelson Rockefeller*
1975   Calkins, Carroll C., et al.   *Story of America*
1975   Reeves, Thomas C.   *Gentleman Boss — The Life of Chester A. Arthur*
1976   Heck, Frank H.   *Proud Kentuckian — John C. Breckinridge 1821–1875*
1976   Sindler, Allan P.   *Unchosen Presidents*
1977   Curtis, Richard   *Vice Presidents — Not Exactly a Crime — Our Vice Presidents from Adams to Agnew*

1977 Abrahamson, Davis *Nixon VS Nixon*

1977 Norwood, Martha F. *Liberty Hall*

1977 Gray, Ralph D. *Gentlemen From Indiana: National Party Candidates* 1836–1940

1977 Laird, Archibald *Monuments Marking the Graves of the Presidents* (Up-dated edition)

1977 Belohlavek, John M. *George Mifflin Dallas —* ` *Jacksonian Patrician*

1977 Libbey, James K. *Alben W. Barkley — Iron Man of Politics*

1978 Engelmayer, Sheldon D., and Wagman, Robert J. *Hubert Humphrey — The Man and His Dream*

1978 Catton, Bruce, and Catton, William B. *The Bold and Magnificent Dream: America's Founding Years 1492–1815*

1978 Manchester, William Raymond *American Caesar — Douglas MacArthur 1880–1964*

1979 Ewy, Marvin *Charles Curtis of Kansas*

PERIODICALS & RELATED PUBLICATIONS

1930   "The Church Pistols"   Chase Manhattan Bank
1955   "Rotary Fifty Years of Service"
1956   "Handbook of the Hall of Fame of New York University"
1959   "In So Little Time"   Creason, Joe, *Louisville Currier Journal Magazine,* Mar. 8
1960-61   "Masonic Facets of the Presidential and Vice Presidential Elections 1788–1930"   Erickson, Jerry R., *Royal Arch Mason Magazine* Vol VI, pp. 11, 12; VII, pp. 1, 2
1961   "Van Buren Grave"   Murphy, George, *Albany Times-Union,* June 25
1968   "An Economic Bill of Rights"   Wallace, Henry A., *Annals of America*
1969   "Guide to Kentucky Historical Highway Markers" Kentucky Historical Society.
1970   "Tribute to Henry A. Wallace"   Offringa, Durk D., Hy-Line International Letter, Pioneer Hi-Bred International, June
1973   "Sir Knight Harry S. Truman"   Rothwell, C.L., *Knight Templar Magazine* Vol. IXX, p. I
1973   "Political Career of the First Adlai E. Stevenson"   Schlup. L.C., University of Illinois
1975   "Stories of Fraternal Patriots"   Masonic Americana, *Knight Templar Magazine,* Sept.
1976   "Hamilton-Burr Dueling Pistols"   Lindsay, Merrill, U.S. Historical Society

1976   "Adlai E. Stevenson and the Gubernatorial Campaign of 1908"   Schlup, Leonard Clarence, *International Review of History and Political Science* Vol. XIII #4

1977   "Adlai E. Stevenson and the 1900 Campaign in Delaware"   Schlup, Leonard Clarence, *Delaware History* Vol. XVII #3

1977   "Adlai E. Stevenson and the Bimetallic Monetary Commission of 1897"   Schlup, Leonard Clarence, *International Review of History and Political Science* Vol XIV #4

1977   "Plan Salute to Wheeler"   *Syracuse Post-Standard,* Mar. 2

1977   "A Look at Malone's Vice President"   *Malone Evening Telegram,* Mar. 2

1979   "Portrait of a Man Called Rocky"   *New York Post Magazine,* Jan. 30, February 5–10.

1979   "Nelson Aldrich Rockefeller: 1908–1979"   *Time,* February 5; "Rocky Recalled" *Time,* February 12.

ENCYCLOPEDIAS

1888   *Appleton's Cyclopedia of American Biography*
1921   *Collier's New Encyclopedia*
1936   *Dictionary of American Biography*
1937   *Standard American Encyclopedia*
1943   *Dictionary of American Biography*
1946–47 *Who's Who in America* Vol. 24
1950   *Columbia Encyclopedia* Second Edition
1960–61 *Who's Who in America* Vol. 31
1975   *New Columbia Encyclopedia*
1976   *Biographical Dictionary*

1977–78   *Who's Who in the East,* 16th Edition
         National Encyclopedia of American Biography Vol. 3
         Dictionary of Biography

DOCUMENTS

1851   Laws of Kentucky, Chapter 462. An Act to authorize the erection of a monument to the memory of Richard Mentor Johnson.

1925–27   Proceedings of the Supreme Council, 33d Degree, Ancient Accepted Scottish Rite, Northern Masonic Jurisdiction.

1965   "A Guide to the Cathedral Church of St. John the Divine," 17th edition, NY

        Denslow, William R., "10,000 Famous Freemasons."

        "History of the Frankfort Cemetery," Frankfort, Kentucky.

1968   Lawing, Hugh A., "Andrew Johnson Historic Site", a revised reprint from The Tennessee Historical Quarterly

PERSONAL INTERVIEWS

1978   Wallace, James W., Sr., Pioneer Hi-Bred International, Des Moines, IA

1978   Wallace, James W., Jr., Pioneer Hi-Bred International, Des Moines, IA

1978   Stark, Byron, Mt. Kenton Cemetery, Paducah, Kentucky

1978   Gurnell, DeWitt S., Dutchess County Historian, Rhinebeck, NY

1978   Offringa, Durk D., Des Moines, IA

1978   Ruland, Clifford L., Principal, Wellsboro Area High School, Wellsboro, PA

ANTHOLOGIES

1900   Stedman, Edmund Clarence   "An American Anthology 1787–1900"

MEMORIAL PARKS

1953   "Pictorial Forest Lawn", Forest Lawn Memorial-Park Association, Inc., Glendale, California

1977   "City of the Dead", Trounstine, Philip J., *The Indianapolis Star,* Spectrum, Section 5, Sunday, June 26

PERSONAL COMMUNICATIONS

Amis, Evelyn S. — Women's Auxiliary to the Dallas County Hospital, Dallas, TX

Barrile, Valerie Francis — Buffalo Rotary Club, Buffalo, NY

Beck, Nancy L. — Office of the Vice President, Washington, DC

Belknap, Ethel G. — Franklin House of History, Malone, NY

Berg, Martha A. — Paducah Rotary Club, Paducah, KY

Bittick, Jane — *Star and Tribune,* Minneapolis, MN

Bobb, Frank W. — Masonic Temple Library, Philadelphia, PA

Conover, Mary L. — Minneapolis, MN

Cross, Leslie H. — National Guard Association of the United States, Washington, DC

Denslow, William R. — *The Royal Arch Mason Magazine,* Trenton, MO

Finney, Carol M. — Texas State Archives, Austin, TX

Frizzell, Robert W. — Illinois Wesleyan University Library, Bloomington, IL

George, Grace M. — Great Falls Historic Landmark, Paterson, NJ

Greene, Lida Lisle, — Iowa State Historical Department, Des Moines, IA

Gillies, S. — New York Historical Society, New York, NY

Gormley, Donald J. — Art Commission of the City of New York, New York, NY

Gurnell, DeWitt S. — Historian of Dutchess County, Rhinebeck, NY

Groe, Beth — Executive Secretary, Des Moines Rotary Club, Des Moines, IA

High, Raymond L. — Bloomington Rotary Club, Bloomington, IL

Hoyer's Photo Supply, Williamsport, PA

Isaac, Tom D. — Rotary Club, Frankfort, KY

Ives, Elizabeth S. — Bloomington, IL

Jackson, Gloria — Library of the Museum of Our National Heritage, Lexington, MA

Jacobs, Jean — National Society, Daughters of the American Revolution, Washington, DC

Jambor, Stephen H. — Rosehill Cemetery, Chicago, IL

Johnson, Judith — The Cathedral Church of St. John the Divine, New York, NY

Jones, Audrey — Christ Church, Capitol Hill, Washington, DC

Kehoe, Barbara B. — Evanston Historical Society, Evanston, IL

Kesilman, Sylvan H. — William Penn Memorial Museum and Archives, Harrisburg, PA

Kincaid, William Alex — Uvalde County Historical Society, Uvalde, TX

Kropp, Sylvia — Green Free Library, Wellsboro, PA

McDowell, Marilyn — Executive Secretary, Lexington Rotary Club, Lexington, KY

McGrath, Frank — Topeka Rotary Club, Topeka, KS

McNally, Wayne — Ludlow Rotary Club, Ludlow, VT

Marchman, Watt P. — Rutherford B. Hayes Library, Freemont, OH

Martignoni, Ava — Commission on Art and Antiquities, U.S. Capitol, Washington, DC

Michaelis, Patricia A. — Kansas State Historical Society, Topeka, KS

Miller, Gail — Georgia Department of Natural Resources, Atlanta, GA

Miller, Susan — Reproduction and Permission Supervisor, *New York Post,* New York, NY

Millonig, Henry — Bicentennial Committee, Old Dutch Church, Kingston, NY

Monaghan, Joanne B. — Bangor Historical Society, Bangor, ME

Nave, Doris B. — Kentucky Historical Society, Frankfort, KY

Niezgodski, Robert C. — Department of City and Bowman Cemeteries, South Bend, IN

Offringa, Durk D. — Des Moines, IA

O'Connor, Joy — Indianapolis, IN

Pankratz, Richard — Kansas State Historical Society, Topeka, KS

Petterchak, Janice — Illinois State Historical Library, Springfield, IL

Phillips, Helen M. — Hi-Bred International, Des Moines, IA

Piriki, Irene L. — Minneapolis Rotary Club, Minneapolis, MN

Preston, Douglas M. — Oneida Historical Society, Utica, NY

Pollard, Steward M. L. — Masonic Service Association, Silver Spring, MD

Porter, L. V. — Evanston Rotary Club, Evanston, IL

Richards, F. Lee — St. Peter's Church, Third and Pine Streets, Philadelphia, PA

Robertson, Ethel — Christ Church, Capitol Hill, Washington, DC

Sanchez, Maria C. — Topeka Cemetery, Topeka, KS

Saunders, Barbara — Georgia Department of Natural Resources, Atlanta, GA

Schlup, Leonard Clarence — Texas Woman's University, Denton, TX

Schweiker, The Honorable Richard S. — U. S. Senator from Pennsylvania

Shaw, Roberta — Green Free Library, Wellsboro, PA

Shoupe, W. Howard — South Bend Rotary Club, South Bend, IN

Spiro Public Library, South Bend, IN
Stahl, Joan — Free Library, Paterson, NJ
Stevenson, The Honorable Adlai E. — U. S. Senator from Illinois
Suits, Jamie — New York State Library, Albany, NY
Tattershall, J. — Franklin House of History, Malone, NY
Thayn, Florian H. — Office of Art, Architect of the Capitol, Washington, DC
Tulk, W. A. — Historical Society of Pennsylvania, Philadelphia, PA
Wachs, Robert F. — Lexington Cemetery, Lexington, KY
Whaley, Fred R. — Forest Lawn Cemetery, Buffalo, NY
Whiteley, Sandy — Northwestern University Library, Evanston, IL
Whitlock, Bev. — *Star and Tribune,* Minneapolis, MN
Whitman, Janice R. — Bangor Historical Society, Bangor, ME
Wright, Michael — Northern Indiana Historical Society, South Bend, IN

LONGEVITY OF THE VICE PRESIDENTS
AGE IN YEARS AT DEATH

50	Tompkins
54	Breckinridge
55	Hobart
56	Arthur
57	Sherman
60	Theodore Roosevelt — Coolidge
61	Colfax
63	Wilson
64	Lyndon B. Johnson
66	Andrew Johnson — Hendricks — Fairbanks — Humphrey
67	King — Wheeler
68	Calhoun
70	Gerry — Richard M. Johnson — Rockefeller
71	Stephens — Tyler — Marshall
72	Clinton — Dallas
74	Fillmore
76	Curtis
77	Wallace
78	Stevenson — Barkley
79	Van Buren
80	Burr
81	Hamlin
83	Jefferson
85	Dawes
88	Truman
90	John Adams
96	Morton
98	Garner

They Passed Away in Their

Fifties	5
Sixties	12
Seventies	14
Eighties	5
Nineties	3

SOME INTERESTING FACTS

Of the 43 men who have served as Vice President, there were:

35 Lawyers
2   Bankers or Financiers
1   Agronomist
1   Cobbler
1   Farmer
1   Pharmacist
1   School Teacher
1   Tailor

Also, of the 43 Vice Presidents,

20 had military service.
19 have inscriptions at the grave or at the cemetery indicating that they had been Vice President.
18 were Master Masons.
10 have statues not located in Statuary Hall in the U.S. Capitol.
7   were elected to the U.S. Senate after having served as Vice President.
6   have their pictures or that of their homes or libraries on a Rotary banner.
5   are buried in cemeteries having an historical marker indicating that a Vice President is buried within its bounds.
5   have a mausoleum as a last resting place.
4   have statues in Statuary Hall in the United States Capitol.
4   attained the rank of Brigadier General
4   were Thirty-Third Degree Masons.
3   were Right Worshipful Grand Masters, F&AM of their native states.
3   were declared traitors.

3 have busts in the New York University Hall of Fame

3 signed the Declaration of Independence.

2 refused to sign the United States Constitution.

2 had a middle initial that did not stand for a middle name.

2 have their faces carved on Mt. Rushmore, the Shrine of Democracy.

2 have Chapter 4, verse 18 from Proverbs carved on their grave monuments.

2 have grave monuments which were paid for by the Federal Government

2 have grave monuments which were paid for by their native states.

2 attained the rank of Major General.

2 were Secretary of War.

2 added a total of 1,500,000 square miles to the territory of the United States without war.

2 founded educational institutions that became universities.

2 resigned as Vice President of the United States.

2 legally had a name other than the one received at birth.

2 received the Gourgas Medal from the Ancient Accepted Scottish Rite, Northern Masonic Jurisdiction.

2 were appointed by a President and approved by Congress.

1 was elected President by the House of Representatives.

1 was elected Vice President by the United States Senate.

1 had his grave monument paid for by a military organization.

1 had his mausoleum donated by the Ancient Accepted Scottish Rite, Northern Masonic Jurisdiction.

1 vigorously opposed having the office of Vice President in the framework of the Executive Branch of the United States Government.

1 was elected but never served.

1 was never elected, but served as Vice President and then as President.

1   has fourteen highway historical markers in his memory.
1   was a member of the Lodge of Elks.
1   was a member of the Independent Order of Odd Fellows.
1   was a member of a Kiwanis Club.
1   was elected an Honorary Member of a Rotary Club.
1   resigned from the office of President.
1   had a memorial plaque erected on his grave by an American Legion Post and another by the independent Order of Odd Fellows and the Rebekahs.
1   lived in the longest frame house in America.
1   was appointed Vice President by a President who had been appointed Vice President.
1   was cremated before burial

2112794

(1)   JOHN ADAMS
April 30, 1789 — March 3, 1797

(Washington — Two Terms)

Elected President 1796

John Adams   Chronology   First Vice President
(Washington   Two Terms)

1735, Oct. 30	Born at Braintree, Massachusetts.
1755	Is graduated from Harvard College.
1756	Studies Law and teaches school at Worcester, Massachusetts.
1758	Admitted to the Bar.
1761	Opposes "Writs of Assistance."
1764, Oct. 25	Marries Abigail Smith. Father of five children.
1765	Leads opposition to Stamp Act.
1768	Opens Law office in Boston.
1770	Wins acquittal for British officer unjustly charged in Boston Massacre.
1774	Delegate to First Continental Congress. Condemns Act that closes Boston Harbor because of the Tea Party.
1775	Delegate to the Second Continental Congress.
1776	Signs the Declaration of Independence.
1778	Commissioner to France.
1779	Member of the Massachusetts Constitutional Convention.
1780	Minister to Holland.
1785	Minister to Great Britain.
1788	Elected Vice President of the United States, first term.
1792	Re-elected Vice President.
1796	Elected President of the United States.
1797, May	First naval vessel of the new Republic launched.

1798	Suspends trade with France. Publicizes the bribe demanded by Talleyrand to have France stop interference with United States commerce with England (XYZ Affair).
1798	Creates Navy Department; establishes the Marine Corps; signs the Alien and Sedition Law which made it illegal to say or print anything of a critical nature about the United States Government.
1799	Refuses to declare war against France. Signs treaty with Cherokee Indians.
1800	Library of Congress established. Fails to be re-elected President of the United States.
1818, Oct. 28	Wife passes away at the age of 73 years.
1820	Member of the Second Massachusetts Constitutional Convention.
1825	Son, John Quincy Adams, elected President of the United States by the House of Representatives.
1826, July 4	Expires at his home in Quincy, Massachusetts at the age of 90 years.
1900	Daughters of the American Revolution affix memorial plaques at the entrance to his last resting place.
	Elected to the New York University Hall of Fame.
1901	Tablet unveiled at the New York University Hall of Fame.
1924	Bust in the Colonnade of the New York University Hall of Fame, by John Francis Paramino, a gift of the Massachusetts Society of the Sons of the Revolution, unveiled.
1950	Immortalized by having silhouette placed on the Quincy Rotary Club banner.
1952	Home at 135 Adams Street, Quincy, Massachusetts designated a National Historic Site.

The grave of John Adams, the first Vice President of the United States, is located in a fourteen-foot square crypt in the basement of the First Parish Church, the Church of the Presidents, Quincy, Massachusetts.

The sarcophagus of John Adams is eight feet long, four feet wide, and four feet high, constructed of grey granite. The top slab, six inches thick, is inscribed:

JOHN ADAMS

A similar sarcophagus to the right of the crypt entrance is inscribed:

ABIGAIL ADAMS

Courtesy of First Parish Unitarian Church, Hancock Street, Quincy, MA.

Tomb of John Adams

Marble plaques at the crypt entrance are inscribed:

JOHN ADAMS
SIGNER OF THE
DECLARATION OF INDEPENDENCE
FRAMER OF THE
CONSTITUTION OF MASSACHUSETTS
SECOND PRESIDENT
OF THE UNITED STATES
1735–1826
THE JOHN ADAMS CHAPTER DAUGHTERS
OF THE
AMERICAN REVOLUTION
CAUSED THIS TABLET
TO BE AFFIXED
1900

ABIGAIL ADAMS
AS DAUGHTER WIFE AND MOTHER
A MODEL OF DOMESTIC WORTH
HER LETTERS ARE AN AMERICAN CLASSIC
1744–1818
THE ABIGAIL ADAMS CHAPTER DAUGHTERS
OF THE
AMERICAN REVOLUTION
CAUSED THIS TABLET
TO BE ERECTED
1900

An impressive marble plaque containing a eulogy to John and Abigail Smith Adams is located near the pulpit of the sanctuary in the Church of the Presidents.

(2)   THOMAS JEFFERSON
March 4, 1797 — March 3, 1801

(John Adams)

Elected President by the House of Representatives 1801

Courtesy of Thomas Jefferson Memorial Foundation, Monticello, VA.

Grave of Thomas Jefferson.

Thomas Jefferson   Chronology   Second Vice President
                        (John Adams)

1743, April 13	Born at Shadwell, Goochland (Albemarle) County, Virginia.
1760	Matriculant, William and Mary College, Williamsburg, Virginia.
1762	Is graduated from William and Mary College. Begins study of Law in the office of George Wythe.
1767	Admitted to the Bar.
1768	Begins construction of Monticello.
1769	Elected to the Virginia House of Burgesses.
1770	Takes up residence at uncompleted Monticello.
1772, Jan. 1	Marries Martha Wayles Skelton. Father of five children.
1773	Member of House of Burgesses.
1774	Publishes protest against British tyranny.
1775	Deputy delegate to Second Continental Congress.
1776	Author of the Declaration of Independence. Signs the document July 4th.
1777	Drafts Act for Religious Freedom in Virginia.
1778	Elected for first of two terms as Governor of Virginia.
1779	Introduces bill against slavery in Virginia.
1781, June	Resigns as Governor of Virginia. Evades capture by British.
1782, Sept. 6	Wife passes away at the age of 33 years.
1783	Virginia Statute for Religious Freedom passed.

1784	Minister to France. Drafts decimal system of coinage.
1785	Designs Capitol to be erected in Richmond, Virginia.
1786	Receives Honorary LLD from Yale.
1787	Receives Honorary LLD from Harvard.
1789	Secretary of State.
1790	Elected member of American Academy of Arts and Sciences.
1791	Receives Honorary LLD from Princeton.
1793	Resigns as Secretary of State.
1796	Elected Vice President of the United States.
1797–1815	President of the American Philosophical Society.
1800	Ties with Aaron Burr in race for the Presidency.
1801, Mar. 4	Begins first term as President after being elected by the House of Representatives on the 36th ballot in February.
1802	War with Tripoli; Army Corps of Engineers created; West Point Military Academy opens. Allows Alien & Sedition Law to expire.
1803	Signs treaty approving the Louisiana Purchase; orders the Lewis and Clark Expedition.
1804	Elected President for a second term under the 12th Amendment to the Constitution.
1805	Successfully concludes the Tripolitan War.
1807	American ship, *Chesapeake,* searched by the British. Orders Embargo.
1808	Signs treaty with Osage Indians.
1809	Retires to Monticello.
1814	Sells personal library to the Library of Congress.*

*The Library of Congress was established in 1800, burned by the British during the War of 1812, and was started again in 1815 with the 6,500 volumes from Jefferson's own library.

1817	Virginia Assembly votes to establish the University of Virginia.
1819	University of Virginia chartered as a state university.
1821	Designs Rotunda and Serpentine Wall for the University.
1825	Becomes Rector of the University as instruction begins.
1826, July 4	Passes away at his home in Monticello. Wills estate to the people of the United States. Age at death 83 years.
1827	Executors contest his will and break it.
1828	Possessions sold to pay his debts.
1883, July 4	Original grave obelisk presented by heirs to the University of Missouri at Columbia, Missouri.
1885, July 4	Grave obelisk dedicated on the campus of the University of Missouri, the first state university to be established in the territory of the Louisiana Purchase.
1900	Elected to the New York University Hall of Fame.
1901	Tablet dedicated at the New York University Hall of Fame.
1923	Thomas Jefferson Memorial Foundation acquires Monticello.
1924	Bust in the Colonnade of the New York University Hall of Fame by Robert Aitken, a gift of the Jefferson Boys' Pilgrimage Committee, unveiled.
1936	Face unveiled on Mount Rushmore Shrine of Democracy Memorial, South Dakota.
1943, April 13	Jefferson Memorial, with heroic statue of Jefferson, dedicated on rim of the Tidal Basin, Washington, D.C.
1955	Monticello, home of Jefferson, appears on the banner of the Charlottesville Rotary Club.

The grave of Thomas Jefferson, the second Vice President of the United States is located at Monticello, Charlottesville, Virginia. The plot is surrounded by an iron fence and is dominated by the obelisk marking his grave.

The granite monument is the second one to be erected at the grave because the inscription on the original was obliterated by wind and rain.

As directed in his will, it is six feet high and carries this inscription:

Here was buried
THOMAS JEFFERSON

Author of the Declaration of Independence
Of the Statute of Virginia for Religious Freedom
And the Father of the University of Virginia
Born April 13, 1743   Died July 4, 1826

The original grave obelisk was dedicated on the campus of the University of Missouri, Columbia, Missouri on July 4, 1885.

(3)　　　AARON BURR
March 4, 1801 — March 3, 1805

(Jefferson — First Term)

Courtesy of Princeton Cemetery. Photograph by Ruth W. Laird

Aaron Burr Grave Monument

1756, Feb. 6	Born at Newark, New Jersey.
1772	Is graduated from the College of New Jersey.
1774	Abandons Theology for Law.
1775	Joins Continental Army.
1776	Captain, Continental Army.
1777	Lieutenant Colonel, Continental Army.
1779	Resigns from Continental Army due to ill health.
1780	Studies Law.
1782	Licensed attorney and counselor-at-law in New Jersey.
1782, July	Marries Theodosia Barstow Prevost. Father of one child.
1783, June 21	Daughter Theodosia born.
	Moves to New York City.
1789	New York State Attorney General.
1791	United States Senator.
1793	Introduces Dorothea Todd to James Madison. In 1794 she becomes Dolley, wife of the fourth President.
1794	First wife expires.
1797	Elected to New York State Assembly.
1799	Establishes the Bank of Manhattan Company.
1800	Ties with Jefferson for U.S. Presidency. Election reverts to House of Representatives. Duels with Colonel John B. Church, owner of custom-built dueling pistols, now owned by the Chase Manhattan Bank.
1801	On the 36th ballot in House of Representatives loses Presidency to Thomas Jefferson.

1804	Contemplates running for Governor of New York.
1804, July 11	Duels with Hamilton at Weehawken, New Jersey. Uses Church pistol.
1804, July 13	Coroner's Jury of New York's leading citizens called to make official inquiry on the death of Alexander Hamilton.
1804, July 28	Jury returns verdict of murder and indicts Nathaniel Pendleton, Hamilton's second, and William Van Ness, Burr's second, as accessories.
1805	Presides during impeachment trial of Chief Justice Chase. Senate votes appreciation of ability in Chase trial.
1805, Mar. 16	Travels to Spanish Territories in the southwest.
1806	Prosecuted in Kentucky for treason. No conviction.
1807, Mar. 30	Arrested and tried for treason by Federal authorities. Acquitted September 1st.
1808, June	Sails for France.
1812, May	Returns to the United States.
1833, July	Marries widow of Stephen Jumel.
1834, July	Second wife institutes suit for divorce.
1836, Sep. 14	Expires at Port Richmond, Staten Island, at the age of 80 years.
1930	Church Pistols, historical relics of the Burr-Hamilton Duel, purchased from the great granddaughter of Colonel John B. Church by the Chase Manhattan Bank.
1962	Kentucky Historical Highway Marker #1158 states that Colonel Joseph Hamilton Daviess, as U.S. Attorney for Kentucky, "prosecuted Aaron Burr in 1806 for treason, in plotting to seize Spanish Territory, a friendly nation; but he did not obtain a conviction."

The grave of Aaron Burr, third Vice President of the United States, is located in the Princeton Cemetery, Princeton, New Jersey. This cemetery, established in 1757, is referred to as the Westminster Abbey of the United States and is owned and administered by the Nassau Presbyterian Church.

The presidents of the college (now Princeton University) occupy the Presidents' Plot near the corner of Witherspoon and Wiggins Streets.

Surrounded on three sides by yew shrubs stands the limestone grave monument of Aaron Burr, Jr. His grave is located at the foot of the grave of his father, Reverendi Admodum Viri Aaronis Burr, first president of the College of New Jersey.*

*The Presidents' Plot is surrounded by a foot-high pipe enclosure and lists the following:

Aaron Burr, Sr.	1748–57	Ashbel Green	1812–22
Jonathan Edwards	1758	James Carnahan	1823–54
Samuel Davies	1759–61	John Maclean	1854–68
Samuel Finley	1761–66	James McCosh	1868–88
John Witherspoon	1768–94	John Grier Hibben	1912–32
Stanhope Smith**	1795–1812	Aaron Burr, Jr.	

**Maternal Grandfather of John Cabell Breckinridge, fourteenth Vice President of the United States.

The badly eroded monument is four feet high, twenty-one inches wide, and eight inches thick. It is supported by a base twenty-six inches wide and eight and one half inches high. The foundation extends six inches above ground, is thirty-one inches wide, and twenty-one inches from front to rear.

The inscription reads:

AARON BURR
BORN FEB 6th 1756
DIED SEPT. 14th 1836
A COLONEL IN THE ARMY OF THE
REVOLUTION
VICE PRESIDENT OF THE UNITED
STATES FROM 1801 to 1805

Courtesy of Princeton Cemetery. Photograph by Ruth W. Laird

Grave of Aaron Burr

(4)   GEORGE CLINTON
March 4, 1805 — April 20, 1812

(Jefferson — Second Term   Madison — First Term)

Died in Office

Courtesy of Library of Congress

George Clinton statue in U.S. Capitol "Hall of Fame."

George Clinton   Chronology   Fourth Vice President
  (Jefferson — Second Term   Madison — First Term)

1739, July 26	Born at Little Britain, Ulster County, New York.
1757	Sailor on Privateer *Defiance*.
1759	Subaltern in expedition against Fort Frontenac. County Clerk.
1763	Begins practice of Law in Albany, New York.
1768	Elected to Provincial Assembly.
1770, Feb. 7	Marries Cornelia Tappen. Father of six children.
1775	Delegate to Second Continental Congress. Brigadier General, New York Militia.
1777	Brigadier General, Continental Army.
1777, July 30	Elected both Governor and Lt. Governor of New York.
1778	Becomes a Master Mason in Warren Lodge #17 F&AM, New York City.
1781	Advocates state sovereignty.
1783	Major General and president of New York State Society of the Cincinnati.
1787	Refuses to sign the United States Constitution.
1789	Candidate for President of the United States.
1791	Secures the election of Aaron Burr to the U.S. Senate.
1792	Candidate for President for the Anti-Federalist Party. Fails to be elected Vice President by 28 electoral votes.
1795	Declines to be a candidate for Governor of New York.

1796	Completes six terms as New York Governor. Fails in third try for the Presidency of the United States.
1801	Begins seventh term as New York Governor.
1804	Elected Vice President for second term of Jefferson.
1808	Fails in fourth try for the Presidency. Is elected Vice President for the first term of Madison.
1812, Apr. 20	Expires in Washington, D.C. and is buried in the Washington Parish Burial Ground (The Congressional Cemetery). First Vice President to pass away in office. Age at death 72 years.
1873	Bronze statue placed in Statuary Hall of the United States Capitol. The statue is six feet, eight inches tall and was executed by Henry Kirke Brown. Signed front base "H. K. Brown, Sculpt. 1873." It is located in the Small House Rotunda. The citation reads:

GEORGE CLINTON, 1739–1812, NEW YORK

Lawyer, soldier, Governor and Vice President. Fought in the French and Indian War and as a Brigadier General in the Revolutionary War; delegate to the Continental Congress, 1775; first Governor of N.Y. 1777–95, 1801–1804; President of the N.Y. convention ratifying the U.S. Constitution; and Vice President of the U.S. under both Jefferson and Madison.

1908, May 30	Reinterred in the cemetery of the Old Dutch Church, Kingston, New York.
1976	Bicentennial plaque unveiled at the grave site by the Bicentennial Committee of the Old Dutch Church.

Photos by George J. Habernig, Kingston, N.Y.

George Clinton Monument
Old Dutch Church Side

George Clinton Monument
Main Street Side

George Clinton Monument
Fair Street Side

George Clinton Monument
Wall Street Side

The monument marking the grave of George Clinton, fourth Vice President of the United States, is located in the cemetery of the Old Dutch Church, Kingston, New York.

The conspicuous memorial is twelve feet high, crowned by a metal torch-shaped finial. The three-tiered foundation and base is seventy-five inches square at ground level and sixty-six inches square at the pedestal. Each tier is approximately nine inches in height. The pedestal is fifty-four inches square and forty inches high. It supports a seven-foot high pyramid. The monument faces Main Street and the front plaque carries this inscription:

TO THE MEMORY OF GEORGE CLINTON
HE WAS BORN IN THE STATE OF NEW YORK
ON THE 26th JULY 1739 AND DIED IN THE
CITY OF WASHINGTON ON THE 20th APRIL 1812
IN THE 73rd YEAR OF HIS AGE.
HE WAS A SOLDIER AND STATESMAN
OF THE REVOLUTION,
EMINENT IN COUNCIL, DISTINGUISHED IN WAR.
HE FILLED WITH UNEXAMPLED
UNSELFISHNESS, PURITY, AND ABILITY
AMONG MANY OTHER HIGH OFFICES,
THOSE OF GOVERNOR OF HIS NATIVE STATE AND
VICE PRESIDENT OF THE UNITED STATES.
WHILE HE LIVED, HIS VIRTUE, WISDOM
AND VALOR WERE THE PRIDE, THE ORNAMENT,
AND THE SECURITY OF HIS COUNTRY, AND WHEN
HE DIED HE LEFT AN ILLUSTRIOUS EXAMPLE OF A
WELL SPENT LIFE,
WORTHY OF ALL IMITATION.
THIS MONUMENT IS AFFECTIONATELY
DEDICATED BY HIS CHILDREN.

Beneath this inscription is an eleven and one half-inch long by eight-inch wide bronze plaque which says:

GEORGE CLINTON
FIRST GOVERNOR OF NEW YORK STATE
1777–1804
VICE PRESIDENT UNITED STATES
1804*–1812
HONORED BY WILWICK CHAPTER
DAR

A metal flag holder at the base of the monument contains the national colors and the initials "A S R 1775."

Courtesy of the Old Dutch Church. Photograph by Ruth W. Laird.

George Clinton Plaque. Erected by the Old Dutch Church Bicentennial Committee, 1976.

The plaque of the pedestal facing Fair Street has, in basso-relievo, a fasces, symbolic of power, emblem of authority.

The basso-relievo of the plaque facing the Old Dutch Church building has a staff with one serpect coiled around it, symbolic of healing.

The plaque facing Wall Street has a winged staff with two serpents coiled around it (a Caduceus), symbolic of Hermes, messenger of the Gods, or Mercury, the ancient herald.

In the lowest section of the pyramid, facing Main Street, is a twenty-inch-in-diameter silhouette of the face of George Clinton. On the opposite side (the rear) are crossed sabres.

At the sidewalk in front of the monument is a forty-inch high and eighteen and one half-inch wide block of polished granite displaying a bronze plaque placed in 1976 by the Old Dutch Church Bicentennial Committee. The Bicentennial plaque reads:

GEORGE CLINTON
BORN JULY 26, 1739, LITTLE BRITAIN, N.Y.
MARRIED FEBRUARY 3, 1770, CORNELIA TAPPEN.
DIED APRIL 20, 1812 BURIED WASHINGTON, D.C.
ULSTER COUNTY CLERK 1759–1812
BRIGADIER GENERAL REVOLUTIONARY WAR
FIRST GOVERNOR NEW YORK STATE
1777–1795   1801–1804
VICE PRESIDENT OF THE UNITED STATES UNDER
JEFFERSON AND MADISON 1804*–1812
BODY AND MONUMENT BROUGHT TO THIS SITE
MAY 30, 1908

*Was elected Vice President in November 1804. Sworn in as Vice President March 4, 1805.

(5)   ELBRIDGE GERRY
March 4, 1813 — November 23, 1814

(Madison — Second Term)

Died in Office

Courtesy of Congressional Cemetery. Photograph by Ruth W. Laird

Elbridge Gerry Grave Monument

Elbridge Gerry   Chronology   Fifth Vice President
                        (Madison   Second Term)

1744, July 17	Born at Marblehead, Massachusetts.
1762	Is graduated from Harvard.
1763	Engaged in Atlantic and Gulf Coast shipping.
1769	Becomes a Master Mason, Philanthropic Lodge F&AM, Marblehead, Massachusetts.
1772	Member Massachusetts General Court.
1774–75	Member Provincial Congresses of Massachusetts.
1776	Signs Declaration of Independence.
1778	Member Second Continental Congress.
1786	Marries Ann Thompson. Father of eight children.
1787	Signs Articles of Confederation; member Constitutional Convention and opposes adoption of office of Vice President.
1788	Publishes views on the new Constitution and refuses to sign the document.
1789–93	U.S. Congressman.
1797	Goes on mission to France; involved in XYZ Affair.
1800	First of five unsuccessful races for Governor of Massachusetts.
1810	Governor of Massachusetts, first term.
1811	Second term as Governor; signs bill creating new election districts, later known as Gerrymander.
1812	Elected Vice President, Madison second term.
1814, Nov. 23	Expires in Washington, DC at age of 70.

1823	Grave monument erected in the Congressional Cemetery and paid for by an Act of Congress. Congress refuses to approve payment of salary of Vice President to widow for the balance of his term.
1976, April	Association for the Preservation of Historic Congressional Cemetery formed.
1977, May	Capitol Hill Restoration Society reaffirms its interest in saving the Congressional Cemetery from further decline and neglect and returning it to a place of beauty and national pride.

The grave of Elbridge Gerry, the fifth Vice President of the United States, is located in the historic Congressional Cemetery, Washington, D.C. It is often called the first American Valhalla. His last resting place is marked by a beautiful marble monument, approximately twelve feet high. It stands at the beginning of a row of Congressional Cenotaphs running at right angles to the cemetery fence paralleling E Street, S.E.

With each side facing the major points of the compass, the monument is a miniature pyramid with a base six feet square, rising to a summit two feet, four and one half inches square.

On this summit an octagonal rests on eight, foot-high colonnettes, symbolizing enduring fame. This, in turn, supports a large hour glass, reminiscent of time. The hour glass has a dome-shaped pediment holding a flame-shaped finial, conveying, symbolically, the message: "His memory shall not die."

The eastern face has this inscription:

THE
TOMB
of
ELBRIDGE GERRY

VICE PRESIDENT
of the
UNITED STATES
Who died suddenly in this city
on his way to the Capitol
NOVEMBER 23, 1814
AGE 70
THUS FULFILLING
HIS OWN MEMORABLE INJUNCTION:
"IT IS THE DUTY OF EVERY CITIZEN, THOUGH
HE MAY HAVE BUT ONE DAY TO LIVE
TO DEVOTE THAT DAY TO THE
GOOD OF HIS COUNTRY."

Courtesy of the Congressional Cemetery. Photograph by Ruth W. Laird

Elbridge Gerry Tomb (Eastern Face)

The western face is inscribed:

ERECTED
By Order
of the CONGRESS of the
UNITED STATES
1823

Courtesy of the Congressional Cemetery. Photograph by Ruth W. Laird.

Elbridge Gerry Tomb (Western Face)

(6)   DANIEL D. TOMPKINS
March 4, 1817 — March 3, 1825

(Monroe — Two Terms)

Photograph by Becket Logan, New York, NY.

Daniel D. Tompkins. Bust and Inscription.

Daniel D. Tompkins   Chronology   Sixth Vice President
            (Monroe   Two Terms)

1774, June 21	Born at Scarsdale, West Chester County, New York.
1791	Adopts middle initial D to distinguish him from a classmate of the same name at Columbia College.
1795	Valedictory oration at graduation from Columbia College most outstanding in the history of the college and university.
1797	Admitted to the Bar and begins practice of Law.
	Marries Hannah Minthorne. Father of seven children.
1800	Becomes a Master Mason in Hiram Lodge #72 F&AM, Mt. Pleasant, New York.
1801	Member New York State Constitutional Convention.
1803	Member New York State Assembly.
1804	Elected to Congress; immediately resigns.
1805	Appointed Associate Justice, New York Supreme Court.
1807	Elected New York Governor and serves four terms.
1812	Prevents chartering of banking institution in New York.
1814	Accepts command of 3d Military District, War of 1812. Pledges personal credit to pay for troops & supplies. Declines office of Secretary of State.

1816	Elected Vice President, first term under Monroe.
1820	Elected Vice President, second term under Monroe.
1820–21	Serves as Right Worshipful Grand Master of the Grand Lodge F&AM of New York.
1825, June 11	Expires at his home on Staten Island at age of 50 years.
1827	Mansion on Staten Island partially destroyed by vandals.
1834	New York City acquires land at East Tenth Street and Avenue B.
1836	Land acquired by New York City at East Tenth Street and Avenue B made a public park.
1878	Tompkins Square Park, two blocks east of Daniel D. Tompkins' last resting place, not officially dedicated to the former New York Governor and two-term Vice President of the United States, recalls to many the memory of the sixth Vice President.
1939	A bust is erected in the West Yard of St. Mark's Church-in-the-Bowery by the United Daughters of 1812 in memory of the sixth Vice President of the United States.
1962	Kentucky Historical Highway Marker #1093 states: "Monroe County-Tompkinsville: The only county of the 2,957 in the United States named for a President where the county seat is named for the contemporary Vice-President. County formed in 1820; named for James Monroe the fifth President, author of the Monroe Doctrine. The country seat named for Daniel Tompkins. Two terms for each covered 1817-25."

The grave of Daniel D. Tompkins is located in the Minthorne vault under the east wall of the St. Mark's Church-in-the-Bowery, Tenth Street at Second Avenue in New York City. The thirty-inch wide and forty-inch high plaque, on the east wall of the church, facing Second Street, reads:

Photograph by Becket Logan, New York, N.Y.

DANIEL D. TOMPKINS,

1774 Aged 51 Years 1825

Governor of the State of New York

1807 — 1817

Vice President of the UNITED STATES

1817   1825

THE WAR OF 1812

ERECTED BY
GOV. DANIEL D. TOMPKINS CHAPTER
U.S.D. 1812

Daniel D. Tompkins. Grave Monument.

SACRED
to the
Memory
of
MANGLE MINTHORNE
who departed
this life
on the 20th day of April
1824
aged 83 years, 8 months
and 6 days

Below the palm leaf is the following:

DANIEL D. TOMKINS
1774　　　Aged 51 years　　　1825
GOVERNOR of the STATE of NEW YORK
1807–1817
VICE PRESIDENT OF THE UNITED STATES
1817　　　　　　1825

Erected by
Gov. Daniel D. Tompkins Chapter
U.S.D. 1812

In the churchyard on the west of the Church, just beyond the
iron fence at the church entrance is a five foot, six-inch high
pedestal that supports a thirty-two by twenty-two-inch bust of
the sixth Vice President of the United States. The inscription
states:

DANIEL D. TOMPKINS
A GREAT AMERICAN
SON OF A REVOLUTIONARY PATRIOT
BORN IN FOX MEADOWS (NOW SCARSDALE) N.Y.
JUNE 21, 1774
DIED IN TOMKINSVILLE, STATEN ISLAND, N.Y.
JUNE 11, 1825
GOVERNOR OF NEW YORK STATE　　　1807–1817

VICE PRESIDENT OF THE UNITED STATES   1817–1825
MILITARY COMMANDER OF THE THIRD MILITARY
DISTRICT OCTOBER 14, 1814
GOVERNOR TOMPKINS SUSTAINED THE CREDIT OF
THE UNITED STATES GOVERNMENT
WITH HIS PERSONAL FUNDS,
AT A TIME WHEN THE BANKS OF
NEW YORK REFUSED TO
LOAN TO THE GOVERNMENT,
ON ITS NOTES WITHOUT HIS ENDORSEMENT.
A GRADUATE OF COLUMBIA COLLEGE 1795
A MEMBER OF THE
STATE CONSTITUTIONAL CONVENTION 1821.
PRESIDENT MADISON HANDED HIM THE PORTFOLIO
OF SECRETARY OF STATE, WHICH HE REFUSED.
FOUNDER OF THE NEW YORK STATE HISTORICAL
SOCIETY AND CHANCELLOR OF THE UNIVERSITY OF
NEW YORK.
DANIEL D. TOMPKINS HELD NOT ONLY THE OFFICE
OF GOVERNOR OF THE STATE,
BUT, WAS PAYMASTER,
QUARTERMASTER, COMMISSARY, AND GENERAL
DISTRIBUTING AGENT FOR THE STATE OF NEW
YORK AND THE UNITED STATES.
ERECTED BY
THE UNITED DAUGHTERS OF 1812
OF THE STATE OF NEW YORK
NOVEMBER 2, 1939

Above the inscription is a circle encompassing the Star and
Anchor together with

NS
U S D
1812

On certain years, a ceremony of remembrance is conducted by the Grand Lodge of Free and Accepted Masons of New York at St. Mark's Church and a wreath laid on the vault of Daniel D. Tompkins, Grand Master of New York Masons 1820–1821.

Photograph by Becket Logan, New York, N.Y.

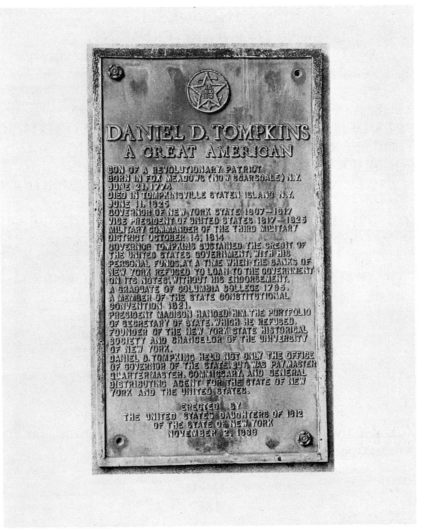

Daniel D. Tompkins. Bust Inscription West Yard.

(7)   JOHN C. CALHOUN
March 4, 1825 — December 28, 1832

(John Quincy Adams   Jackson — First Term)

Resigned as Vice President before term expired

Courtesy of Library of Congress.

John Caldwell Calhoun statue in U.S. Capitol "Hall of Fame."

John Caldwell Calhoun   Chronology   Seventh Vice President
    (John Quincy Adams   Jackson — First Term)

1782, Mar. 18	Born in Calhoun Settlement, South Carolina.
1804	Is graduated from Yale.
1805	Studies Law in Litchfield, Connecticut.
1807	Opens Law office in Abbeville, South Carolina.
1808	Elected to South Carolina Legislature.
1810	Elected to U.S. Congress.
1811, Jan.	Marries Floride Calhoun. Father of one child.
1812	Recommends declaration of war against Great Britain.
1817	Appointed Secretary of War by President Monroe.
1819	Threatens General Jackson with court-martial.
1824	Elected Vice President under John Quincy Adams.
1828	Elected Vice President, first term Andrew Jackson.
1832	Directs passage of famous South Carolina Ordinance of Nullification.
1832, Dec.	Resigns as Vice President.
1833	Appointed to the U.S. Senate.
1835	Leads Senate opposition to accepting the legacy of James Smithson to the United States for the founding of the Smithsonian Institution.
1844, Mar.	Appointed Secretary of State by President Tyler.
1845	Completes admission of Texas negotiations as slave state.
	Appointed U.S. Senator.

1846	Opposes war with Mexico.
1849	Rejects Wilmot Proviso.
1850, Mar. 4	Last formal speech read in Senate.
1850, Mar. 31	Expires in Washington, DC. Interred in Congressional Cemetery. Age 68. Latrobe Cenotaph there commemorates his passing.
1884	State of South Carolina erects monument over his grave in St. Philip's Church cemetery, Charleston, South Carolina.
1893	Clemson Agricultural College opens on his former plantation.
1910	Marble statue placed in Statuary Hall of U.S. Capitol to represent South Carolina. The marble statue is seven feet seven inches in height. It was produced by Frederic W. Ruckstuhl. Signed right base "F. W. RUCKSTUHL, S.C./1909." The citation:

JOHN C. CALHOUN, 1782–1850, South Carolina. Lawyer, statesman, orator and Vice President of the United States; leader of a school of earnest men who believed secession was warranted or at least permissible under the Constitution of the United States because not expressly forbidden. State House of Representatives 1808–09; U.S. House of Representatives 1811–17; Secretary of War 1817–25; Vice President 1825–32; U.S. Senator 1832–43; 1845–50; Secretary of State 1844–45.

It is located in East Central Hall.

The monument marking the grave of John Caldwell Calhoun, seventh Vice President of the United States, is a massive granite sarcophagus ten feet long, six feet wide, and nine feet high. It rests on a stone floor fifteen feet two inches long and ten feet two inches wide. Both ends of the capstone are supported by polished granite pillars three and one half feet long.

The south side of the monument has this inscription:

JOHN CALDWELL CALHOUN
BORN MARCH 8, 1782
DIED MARCH 31, 1850

The east side is inscribed:

REPRESENTATIVE
IN THE LEGISLATURE
MEMBER
OF CONGRESS
UNITED STATES
SENATOR

The north side is inscribed:

ERECTED
BY THE STATE OF
SOUTH CAROLINA
AD 1884

The west side carries the following:

SECRETARY
OF WAR
VICE PRESIDENT
SECRETARY
OF
STATE

Courtesy of St. Philip's Church. Photograph by Ruth W. Laird

John C. Calhoun Sarcophagus (North Side)

Courtesy of the Congressional Cemetery. Photograph by Ruth W. Laird

Calhoun Latrobe Cenotaph

Courtesy of St. Philip's Church.
Photograph by Ruth W. Laird.

Courtesy of St. Philip's Church.
Photograph by Ruth W. Laird.

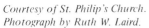

John C. Calhoun Sarcophagus.
(West and South Sides)

John C. Calhoun Sarcophagus (East Side)

Senator Calhoun's grave is located in St. Philip's Protestant Episcopal Church graveyard, 146 Church Street, Charleston, South Carolina.

The senator passed away in Washington, D.C.; a Latrobe Cenotaph stands along the avenue leading to the chapel from E Street, S.E. in the Congressional Cemetery and bears this inscription:

THE HONORABLE
JOHN C. CALHOUN
A SENATOR IN THE
CONGRESS OF THE
UNITED STATES
FROM THE STATE OF
SOUTH CAROLINA
BORN
DIED 31ST MARCH 1850

Calhoun's only child was buried in the Congressional Cemetery in 1820.

(8)   MARTIN VAN BUREN
March 4, 1833 — March 3, 1837

(Jackson — Second Term)

Elected President in 1836

Courtesy of Kinderhook Cemetery. Photograph by Ruth W. Laird

Martin Van Buren Grave Monument

Martin Van Buren   Chronology   Eighth Vice President
          (Andrew Jackson   Second Term)

1782, Dec. 5	Born at Kinderhook, New York.
1796	Begins informal study of law.
1803	Admitted to the Bar.
1807, Feb. 21	Marries Hannah Hoes. Father of four children. Counselor of New York Supreme Court.
1808	Appointed Surrogate of Columbia County, New York.
1813	New York State Senator.
1815	State Attorney General; Regent, State University of New York.
1819, Feb. 5	Wife passes away.
1821	United States Senator; resigns in 1828.
1828	Elected Governor of New York. Resigns 1829.
1829	Appointed Secretary of State. Resigns 1831.
1831	Appointed Minister to Great Britain.
1832	Ministerial appointment not confirmed by U.S. Senate.
	Elected Vice President of the United States.
1836	Elected President of the United States. Contemporary Vice President has to be elected by the Senate.
1837	Signs agreement with Seminole Indians; signs Chippewa Indian Treaty; Chief Osceola seized under flag of truce and imprisoned; Seminole Indians defeated in battle.
1839	Aroostook War.
1840	Opposes annexation of Texas; fails to be re-elected President.

1844	Fails to be nominated for President by Democrats.
1848	Fails to be nominated for President by Free Soil Party.
1862, July 24	Passes away at his home in Kinderhook, New York at age of 79 years.
1961, June 25	*Albany Times Union* publishes a letter to the editor from thirty-two sixth graders who described the condition of the eighth President's grave and the shameful display of neglect by the citizens of America toward their eighth president.

Photograph courtesy of Joseph H. Schantz, Kinderhook, N.Y.

Lindenvald, Home of Martin Van Buren, built in 1797.

The grave of Martin Van Buren, eighth Vice President of the United States, is located in the Village Cemetery, Kinderhook, New York.

The twelve-foot high monument is a grey granite obelisk with a four-foot square base fifteen inches high. The shaft measures twenty-five and one half inches square at the base and tapers to one foot square at the summit.

The west side carries this inscription:

MARTIN VAN BUREN
VIIIth PRESIDENT
OF THE UNITED STATES
BORN DEC. 5, 1782
DIED JULY 24, 1862

HANNAH VAN BUREN
HIS WIFE
BORN MAR. 8, 1783
DIED AT ALBANY, N.Y.
FEB. 5, 1819

(Her body was moved to the Kinderhook Cemetery in 1855.)

The south side of the shaft is inscribed:

MARTIN, SON OF MARTIN
AND HANNAH VAN BUREN
BORN DEC. 30, 1812
DIED AT PARIS, FRANCE
MAR. 19, 1855

Three headstones, each fourteen inches high and one foot wide, are located behind the obelisk and are lettered, from left to right,

MVB   HVB   MVB, JR.

In front of the HVB headstone and extending to the base of the obelisk are four flat marble slabs, flush with the turf, which carry the following:

Slab #1

She was a sincere Christian
dutiful child, tender mother
and most affectionate wife,
Precious shall be the memory of her virtues.

Slab #2

Sacred
To the memory of
Mrs. Hannah Van Buren
Wife of
Martin Van Buren
who departed this life
on the 5th of February
AD 1819 in the 36th
year of her
age.

Slab #3

Beneath this tomb
rests the remains of
the first person intered
in this cemetery
Removed to this place
from Albany in 1855.

Slab #4

Blessed are the dead which
die in the Lord from hence-
forth; Yea saith the Spirit,
that they may rest from
their labours; and their
works do follow them.

Darling, Sculpt.
Hudson

(9)   RICHARD MENTOR JOHNSON
March 4, 1837 — March 3, 1841

(Van Buren)

Elected Vice President by the United States Senate, 1837

Courtesy of Frankfort Cemetery. Photograph by Ruth W. Laird

Grave of Richard Mentor Johnson (West Panel)

Richard Mentor Johnson   Chronology   Ninth Vice President
(Van Buren)

1781, Oct. 17	Born at Bryant's Station, Scott County (Beargrass), Kentucky.
1796	Studies Latin.
1800	Student Transylvania University.
1802	Admitted to the Bar.
	Made a Master Mason in Hiram Lodge #4, F&AM, Frankfort, Kentucky.
1804	Elected to the Kentucky State Legislature.
1806	Elected to the United States House of Representatives.
1812	Introduces resolutions in Congress to establish a Naval Academy; organizes Columbian College (now George Washington University); founds Georgetown College in Kentucky.
1812–14	Colonel Kentucky Rifles; wounded in Battle of the Thames; kills Tecumseh; earns title "Father of American Cavalry."
1815	Returns to Congress.
1818, Apr. 4	Congressional Resolution Citation includes presentation of sword for valor in battle.
1819	Elected to the U.S. Senate.
1825	Gives his Blue Springs Farm to the United States Government to establish the Choctaw Academy, the first school for the education of Indians.
1829	Elected to the House of Representatives of Kentucky.

1837	Elected Vice President of the United States, in lieu of majority of Electoral votes for the office, by the Senate.
1840	Fails to be re-elected Vice President.
1841	Elected to the Kentucky House of Representatives.
1850	Re-elected to the Kentucky House of Representatives.
1850, Nov. 19	Passes away in Frankfort, Kentucky at the age of 70 years.
1851, Mar. 15	General Assembly of the Commonwealth of Kentucky appropriates $900 and appoints a commission to erect a monument over his grave.
1856	Grave monument designed by Robert E. Launitz unveiled.
1862	Kentucky Historical Highway markers:
	#741 Notes that he was one of four Kentuckians to be elected Vice President of the United States.
	#739 Commemorates his birthplace.
	#125 Located at Paintsville, notes that Johnson County was named in his honor.
	#185 Notes that he attended a reunion of the survivors of the Battle of the Thames October 5, 1836, at the historic tavern in Harrodsburg, when he was Vice President.
	#135 Notes that his home became the first Indian school in the United States in 1825.

The grave of Richard Mentor Johnson, ninth Vice President of the United States, is located at the extreme southern point of the military mound in the Frankfort Cemetery, Frankfort, Kentucky. The plot is surrounded by a thirty-two-inch high iron picket fence.

Courtesy of Frankfort Cemetery. Photographs by Ruth W. Laird

Colonel Johnson Killing Tecumseh (South Panel)

Courtesy of Frankfort Cemetery

North Panel with Face of Richard M. Johnson

A granite foundation six feet five inches square and one foot high supports an Italian marble pedestal five feet five inches high. This pedestal is demarcated by an upright cannon at each corner. Above the pedestal, a cap supports a ten-foot high broken column, whose top is enfolded by a flag of stars and stripes. It is crowned by an American eagle, facing west, holding a laurel wreath in its beak.

The entire monument, considered the most beautiful and impressive in the United States, is adorned by symbolic sculpture.

The east panel carries this inscription, in one-inch high letters:

RICHARD MENTOR JOHNSON
BORN AT
BRYANT'S STATION, KENTUCKY
ON THE 17th DAY OF OCTOBER
1781
DIED IN
FRANKFORT, KENTUCKY
ON THE
19th DAY OF NOVEMBER
1850

Courtesy of Frankfort Cemetery. Photograph by Ruth W. Laird

East Panel Inscription of Richard M. Johnson Grave Monument

Robert E. Launitz of New York, a master in cemetery sculpture, designed and executed the work. The erosion of time, the elements, and vandals have not marred its beauty.

The face of Johnson, in bas-relief, occupies the north panel. The shield at the base of the column above has fifteen stars.

On the south panel, Colonel Johnson is depicted on horseback in the act of killing Tecumseh. At the base of the column above are the arms of Kentucky surrounded by branches of oak and laurel.

The inscription on the west panel reads:

TO THE MEMORY OF
COLONEL RICHARD M. JOHNSON.
A FAITHFUL PUBLIC SERVANT
FOR NEARLY HALF A CENTURY, AS A MEMBER
OF THE KENTUCKY LEGISLATURE AND
REPRESENTATIVE AND SENATOR IN CONGRESS.
AUTHOR OF THE SUNDAY MAIL REPORT
AND OF THE LAWS ABOLISHING IMPRISONMENT
FOR DEBT IN KENTUCKY
AND IN THE UNITED STATES;
DISTINGUISHED FOR HIS VALOUR
AS COLONEL OF A KENTUCKY REGIMENT
IN THE BATTLE OF THE THAMES.
FOR FOUR YEARS VICE PRESIDENT
OF THE UNITED STATES
KENTUCKY, HIS NATIVE STATE,
TO MARK THE SENSE OF HIS EMINENT SERVICES
IN THE CABINET AND IN THE FIELD
HAS ERECTED THIS MONUMENT
IN THE RESTING PLACE OF
HER ILLUSTRIOUS DEAD.

The adjoining burial plot south of the Vice President's grave is that of Theodore O'Hara, author of the immortal poem "The Bivouac of the Dead." Theodore O'Hara (1820–1867) had his grave monument erected by the Kentucky State Historical Society in 1913. It carries the following verses:

"THE MUFFLED DRUMS SAD ROLL HAS BEAT
  THE SOLDIER'S LAST TATTOO;
  NO MORE ON LIFE'S PARADE SHALL MEET
  THAT BRAVE AND FALLEN FEW;
  ON FAME'S ETERNAL CAMPING GROUND
  THEIR SILENT TENTS ARE SPREAD,
  AND GLORY GUARDS, WITH SOLEMN ROUND,
  THE BIVOUAC OF THE DEAD.

"REST ON, EMBALMED AND SAINTED DEAD,
  DEAR AS THE BLOOD YE GAVE;
  NO IMPIOUS FOOTSTEP HERE SHALL TREAD
  THE VERBAGE OF YOUR GRAVE;
  NOR SHALL YOUR GLORY BE FORGOT
  WHILE FAME HER RECORD KEEPS,
  OR HONOR POINTS THE HALLOWED SPOT
  WHERE VALOR PROUDLY SLEEPS.

"YON MARBLE MINSTREL'S VOICEFUL STONE
  IN DEATHLESS SONG SHALL TELL,
  WHEN MANY A VANISHED YEAR HATH FLOWN,
  THE STORY HOW YE FELL;
  NOR WRECK, NOR CHANGE, NOR WINTER'S BLIGHT
  NOR TIMES REMORSELESS DOOM,
  CAN DIM ONE RAY OF HOLY LIGHT
  THAT GILDS YOUR GLORIOUS TOMB."

Courtesy of Frankfort Cemetery. Ruth W. Laird photograph

Grave Monument of Theodore O'Hara

Courtesy of Emily Tyler, Charles City County, Sherwood Forest, Virginia.

Sherwood Forest. Home of John Tyler.

JOHN TYLER
March 4, 1841 — April 4, 1841

(William Henry Harrison)

Succeeded to the Presidency upon death of W. H. Harrison
Declared a Traitor

Courtesy of Hollywood Cemetery, Richmond, Va. Ruth W. Laird Photo.

John Tyler Grave Monument.

| John Tyler | Chronology | Tenth Vice President |
| | (William Henry Harrison) | |

1790, Mar. 29	Born in Charles City County, Virginia.
1807	Is graduated from William and Mary College.
1809	Admitted to the Bar.
1811	Member Virginia House of Delegates.
1813, Mar. 29	Marries Letitia Christian. Father of eight children.
	Captain, Virginia Militia, War of 1812.
1817	Begins first of two terms as U.S. Congressman.
1821	Chancellor, William and Mary College.
1823	Virginia House of Delegates.
1825	Governor of Virginia.
1827	United States Senator.
1835	Elected President Pro-Tempore of Senate.
1836	Resigns from Senate rather than vote to expunge the censure of General Jackson from the Senate record.
1838	President of the Virginia African Colonization Society.
1839	Virginia House of Delegates.
1841, Mar. 4	Vice President of the United States.
1841, April 6	Takes oath as President and establishes the principle of Presidential succession.
1841, Sep.	Cabinet resigns.
1842, Sep. 10	First wife expires. Purchases "Sherwood Forest."
1844, Feb. 28	*USS Princeton,* first propeller driven warship, explodes.

1844, June 6	Marries Julia Gardiner. Father of seven children.
	Recommends annexation of Texas.
1859	Chancellor of William and Mary College.
1861, Mar.	Member of Virginia Secession Convention; advocates secession of Virginia from the Union.
1861	Member of Confederate States House of Representatives.
1862, Jan. 18	Passes away in Richmond at the age of 71 years.
1912, Aug. 24	U.S. Congress provides funds to erect a monument marking his grave in the Hollywood Cemetery, Richmond, Virginia.
1967, Feb. 23	The ratification of the 25th Constitutional Amendment clarifies the vague wording of Article 11, Section One that created a bitter controversy when Tyler assumed the office of President in April 1841. It clearly states: "In case of removal of the President from office or of his death, or resignation, the Vice President shall become President."
1968	A National Historic Landmark, Sherwood Forest is the longest frame house in America, 300 feet long, built in 1730 and renovated by President Tyler in 1844.

The monument marking the grave of John Tyler, tenth Vice President of the United States, is located in a plot which measures twenty-seven feet, eight inches along the Presidents' Circle Road in the Hollywood Cemetery, Richmond, Virginia.

The north and south borders of the plot extend westward thirty-two feet, inclining toward each other until they reach the circumference of the James Monroe plot. At this point, the measurement is nine feet, ten inches.

A monolithic granite shaft occupies the front and northern

portion of the Tyler plot. The shaft is twenty-five feet high and is crowned by a bronze Greek urn supported by two American eagles. An heroic bust in bronze of the Vice President, facing east, rests on a pedestal. Beneath the bust is this inscription:

JOHN TYLER
PRESIDENT
OF THE
UNITED STATES
1841–1845
BORN
IN CHARLES CITY COUNTY
MARCH 29, 1790
DIED
IN THE CITY OF RICHMOND
JANUARY 18, 1862

On the north side of the monolith is a bas-relief of a male figure bearing a shield containing the seals of the United States and the state of Virginia in the left hand, significant of his relations with the National Government and his native state.

The hand of the extended right arm holds faggots.

The bas-relief on the south side carries a draped female figure representing memory. She holds a laurel wreath in the left hand. The right hand is symbolically cultivating the young tree of the Republic, which, during Tyler's administration, began to grow and expand in an exceptional manner.

Beneath the bas-relief on the north face of the paneled monolith is this inscription:

Erected by the Congress of the United States
MCMXV

A flag holder in front of the President Tyler monument states:

IN HONOR OF SERVICE
IN THE WAR OF 1812
JOHN TYLER

Members of the Tyler Family buried in the President Tyler plot, in addition to President John Tyler and Julia Gardiner Tyler, are:

Julia Tyler	Robert L. Tyler
William Wallace	Henry Tyler
Anne B. Tyler	Lyon G. Tyler, Sr.
Lachan Tyler	Mrs. Pearl Tyler Ellis

West of the President Tyler monument is a stone which records that:

> JULIA TYLER DIED 2nd
> MONDAY IN MAY 1871
> Age 21
> OF SUCH IS THE KINGDOM OF HEAVEN

The inscription on the west side of the monument reads:

> PRESIDENT JOHN TYLER
> MARRIED FIRST
> LETITIA CHRISTIAN
> BORN NOVEMBER 12, 1790
> DIED SEPTEMBER 10, 1842
> INTERRED AT CEDAR GROVE
> NEW KENT COUNTY, VA.
> MARRIED SECOND
> JULIA GARDINER
> BORN JULY 23, 1820
> DIED JULY 10, 1889
> INTERRED BY HIS SIDE
> UNDER THIS MONUMENT.

The John Tyler monument was financed by an Act of Congress August 24, 1912. It was unveiled October 12, 1915.

(11)   GEORGE MIFFLIN DALLAS
March 4, 1845 — March 3, 1849

(Polk)

Courtesy of St. Peter's Church. Photograph by Ruth W. Laird

Grave of George Mifflin Dallas

George Mifflin Dallas   Chronology
Eleventh Vice President
(Polk)

1792, July 10	Born at Philadelphia.
1808	Attends Friend's School in Philadelphia.
1810	Is graduated from Princeton.
1812	Admitted to the Bar. Member of the Militia; reaches rank of Major.
1813	Private secretary to Albert Gallatin, Minister to Russia.
1816, May 23	Marries Sophia Chew Nicklin. Father of eight children.
1818	Becomes a Master Mason, Franklin Lodge #134, F&AM, Philadelphia, Pennsylvania.
1827	Mayor of Philadelphia.
1829	District Attorney.
1831	Appointed to the U.S. Senate.
1833	Appointed Attorney General of Pennsylvania.
1834–36	Right Worshipful Grand Master, Grand Lodge of Pennsylvania, Free & Accepted Masons.
1835	State of Pennsylvania investigates the Masonic Fraternal Organization.
1837–39	Minister to Russia.
1844	Elected Vice President of the United States.
1846	Dallas, Texas named in his honor.
1848	Fails to be named as nominee for President or Vice President.
1856	Minister to Great Britain.
1857	Is awarded Honorary Degree by Oxford University.
1861	Recalled from London by President Lincoln.
1863	Railroad president.
1864, Dec. 31	Expires in Philadelphia at the age of 72 years.

The grave of George Mifflin Dallas, the eleventh Vice President of the United States, is located in the cemetery of the Saint Peter's Church, Third and Pine Streets, Philadelphia, Pennsylvania. The grave monument is a flat, white marble slab seven feet four and one half inches long, thirty-four inches wide, and four and one half inches thick. The head of the memorial ledger is north at the southeast corner of the church building.

The inscriptions are as follows:

GEORGE MIFFLIN DALLAS
BORN JULY 10, 1792   DIED DEC. 31, 1864
PHILIP NICKLIN DALLAS
BORN AUG. 13, 1825   DIED MARCH 14, 1866
SOPHIA CHEW DALLAS
BORN JUNE 25, 1798   DIED JAN. 11, 1869
CARY SANDERS DIXON
BORN NOV. 23, 1871   DIED JULY 4, 1872
CATHERINE DALLAS
WIFE OF F. E. DIXON
BORN NOV. 27, 1827   DIED AUG. 18, 1878
FITZ EUGENE DIXON
BORN DEC. 4, 1822   DIED JAN. 22, 1880
JULIA DALLAS
BORN AUG. 25, 1819   DIED JULY 2, 1886
SUSAN DALLAS
BORN FEB. 8, 1831   DIED FEB. 25, 1897
SOPHIA DALLAS
BORN SEPT. 9, 1823   DIED JAN. 7, 1899
WILLIAM BOULTON DIXON
BORN MAY 16, 1860   DIED SEPT. 24, 1892
MARGRETTA SERGEANT DIXON
WIFE OF A. J. DIXON
BORN FEB. 24, 1856   DIED SEPT. 20, 1925
A. J. DALLAS DIXON
BORN OCT. 4, 1850   DIED JUNE 9, 1948

Courtesy of St. Peter's Church. Photograph by Ruth W. Laird

Memorial Ledger showing dates of birth and death of Vice President and Mrs. George Mifflin Dallas.

(12)   MILLARD FILLMORE
March 5, 1849 — July 9, 1850

(Taylor)

Succeeded to the Presidency upon death of Taylor

Courtesy of Forest Lawn Cemetery. Buffalo, New York.

Millard Fillmore Grave Monument.

Millard Fillmore   Chronology   Twelfth Vice President
(Taylor)

1800, Jan. 7	Born at Locke, Cayuga, New York.
1815	Apprenticed to wool carder.
1818	Teaches country school at Scott, New York,
1821	Reads and studies Law in Buffalo.
1823	Admitted to the Bar.
1826, Feb. 5	Marries Abigail Powers. Father of two children.
1829	Member of New York State Assembly.
1833	Member of U.S. House of Representatives until 1835.
1837	Member of U.S. House of Representatives until 1843.
1840	Obtains appropriation for Samuel F. B. Morse telegraph.
1844	Unsuccessful candidate for Governor of New York and for Vice President.
1846	Chancellor of the University of Buffalo.
1847	Commander of Home Guard Mexican War.
1848	Comptroller of State of New York. Elected Vice President.
1850, July 9	Succeeds to the Presidency. Signs Fugitive Slave Law.
1852	Authorizes Commodore Perry Expedition to Japan
	Fails to be nominated for the office of President.
	Approves Trade Treaty with Japan.
1853, Mar. 30	First wife passes away.

1856	Unsuccessful candidate on the American Party ticket for President.
1858, Feb. 10	Marries Caroline Carmichael McIntosh.
1865	One of the founders of the Buffalo Historical Society.
1873	Founds Buffalo General Hospital and the Buffalo SPCA.
1874, Mar. 8	Expires at his home in Buffalo, New York at the age of 74 years.
1932	Life-sized statue unveiled at southeast corner of Buffalo City Hall on Niagara Square.

The pedestal of the Millard Fillmore statue in Niagara Square, Buffalo, New York has this inscription:

MILLARD FILLMORE
1800–1874
THIRTEENTH PRESIDENT OF
THE UNITED STATES
LAWYER
EDUCATOR
PHILANTHROPIST
STATESMAN

The Bronze Plaque on the pedestal under the bust of Millard Fillmore in the Buffalo City Hall has this inscription:

MILLARD FILLMORE
Thirteenth President of
the United States
1850–1853

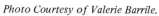

Photo Courtesy of Valerie Barrile.

Millard Fillmore Bust, City Hall, Buffalo, New York

The monument marking the grave of Millard Fillmore, twelfth Vice President of the United States, is located in the Forest Lawn Cemetery, Buffalo, New York. The Fillmore plot is surrounded by an iron fence. In the center of the plot is a shaft of Scotch pink granite on which the following is inscribed:

On the front of the monument:

MILLARD FILLMORE
BORN
JANUARY 7, 1800
DIED
MARCH 8, 1874

On the base:

FILLMORE

On the right side:

ABIGAIL POWERS
FILLMORE
WIFE OF
MILLARD FILLMORE
BORN MARCH 13, 1798
DIED MARCH 30, 1853

On the rear of the monument:

MILLARD POWERS FILLMORE
BORN
APRIL 25, 1828
DIED NOVEMBER 15, 1889
MARY ABIGAIL FILLMORE
BORN
MARCH 27, 1832
DIED JULY 26, 1854

Photo by Valerie Barrile

Millard Fillmore Statue, Niagara Square, Buffalo, New York

On the left side:

CAROLINE CARMICHAEL
WIFE OF
MILLARD FILLMORE
BORN OCT. 21, 1813
DIED AUG. 11, 1881

A bronze plaque on the metal fence enclosure reads:

IN MEMORY
OF
MILLARD FILLMORE
13th PRESIDENT OF THE
UNITED STATES OF AMERICA
BORN JANUARY 7, 1800　　　DIED MARCH 8, 1874
Dedicated by the Millard Fillmore Republican
Woman's Club
Memorial Day May 30, 1932

A simple granite memorial marker bears the letters "M F" indicating the grave of President Fillmore.

(13)   WILLIAM RUFUS de VANE KING
March 4, 1853 — April 18, 1853

(Pierce)

Was sworn in as Vice President in Cuba
but died before reaching Washington, DC.
Never served as Vice President.

Courtesy of Live Oak Cemetery. Ruth W. Laird Photograph.

William Rufus de Vane King Mausoleum.

William Rufus de Vane King   Chronology
              Thirteenth Vice President
                  (Franklin Pierce)

1786, Apr. 7	Born in Sampson County, North Carolina.
1803	Is graduated from the University of North Carolina.
1806	Admitted to the Bar.
1807	Becomes a Master Mason, Phoenix Lodge #8, F&AM, Fayetteville, North Carolina.
	North Carolina State Legislator through 1809.
1811	U.S. Congressman from North Carolina.
1816	Resigns as Congressman to accompany William Pinkney to Naples and St. Petersburg.
1818	Returns to the United States, settles in Alabama; founds and names city of Selma.
1819	U.S. Senator from Alabama; serves until 1844.
1836–40	President Pro-Tempore of Senate.
1844	Minister to France.
1846	Returns to the United States.
1848	Appointed to the U.S. Senate.
1850	President Pro-Tempore of Senate.
1852, Nov.	Elected Vice President of the United States.
	Resigns from Senate to regain health in Cuba.
1853, Mar. 4	Takes oath of Vice President in Cuba under special Act of Congress.
1853, April 18	Expires at his plantation home "King's Bend", the day after he had returned from Cuba. Age 67 years.
1978	Oil painting of Vice President King hangs in the reading room of the Public Library of Selma and Dallas County, 1103 Selma Avenue, Selma, Alabama.

The monument marking the grave of William Rufus de Vane King is located in the Live Oak Cemetery, Selma, Alabama. It is a small free standing building with unimpressive proportions. The white marble mausoleum is eight feet long, eight feet wide, and eight feet high. In the center front is a black iron door two feet eleven inches wide and five feet high. The nine-inch wide lintel carries the following:

HON. WILLIAM R. KING
Vice President of the United States
Died 18th April 1853, aged 67 years
and 11 days

J. T. Allen

On the avenue in front of the King mausoleum is an Alabama Historical Marker which reads:

WILLIAM RUFUS de VANE KING

1786 - 1853

Native Sampson County. North Carolina.
Admitted to bar, 1806. North Carolina House
of Commons 1807-1809. U. S. Congressman 1811-1816
Secretary U. S. Legation Naples and
St. Petersburg 1816-1818.

Moved to Dallas County, Alabama, 1818.
A founder of Selma; named city. Delegate
Alabama Constitutional Convention 1819.
U. S. Senator 1819-1844, 1848-1853.
U. S. Minister to France 1844-1846.
President pro tempore U. S. Senate 1836-1840.
1850-1852. Vice President of
United States, 1853.

ALABAMA HISTORICAL ASSOCIATION

Courtesy of the Live Oak Cemetery. Photographs by Ruth W. Laird

Live Oak Cemetery. Alabama Historical Marker.

Courtesy of the Live Oak Cemetery

Wm. R. D. King. Alabama Historical Marker.

Just beyond the King mausoleum stands an Alabama Historical marker which has this inscription:

LIVE OAK CEMETERY
East portion reserved for graveyard, 1829; west
part purchased City of Selma, 1877. Here are buried:
William Rufus King, 1786–1853, Vice President
of U.S. 1853
John Tyler Morgan, 1824–1907, U.S. Senator,
Brig. Gen. C.S.A.
Edmund Winston Pettus, 1821–1907, U.S. Senator
Brig. Gen. C.S.A.
Nathaniel H. R. Dawson, 1829–1895, U.S.
Commissioner of Education.
William J. Hardee, 1815–1873, Lt. Gen. C.S.A.,
author "Hardee's Tactics."
Catesby 'ap Roger Jones, 1821–1877, Commander
C.S.N., commanded Virginia (Merrimac) in battle
with Monitor 1862.
Robert W. Barnwell, 1849–1902, Episcopal Bishop
of Alabama.
Alabama Historical Association

(14)   JOHN CABELL BRECKINRIDGE
March 4, 1857 — March 3, 1861

(Buchanan)

Was declared a traitor by the U.S. Senate in 1861
Was granted amnesty in 1868

Photograph by Robert F. Wachs

John Cabell Breckinridge Grave Monument

John Cabell Breckinridge   Chronology
Fourteenth Vice President
(Buchanan)

1821, Jan. 15	Born at Thorn Hill, Lexington, Kentucky.
1832	Enrolls in preparatory department, Centre College, Danville, Kentucky.
1835	Becomes a member of the Deinologian Literary Society devoted to orations and debates.
1838	Bachelor of Arts, Centre College.
1839	Graduate student, Princeton, where maternal grandfather, Stanhope Smith, had been president 1795–1812.
1841	Is graduated from Transylvania School of Law.
1841–43	Practices Law in Burlington, Iowa.
1842	Becomes a Master Mason, Des Moines Lodge #41 F&AM, Des Moines, Iowa.
1843, Dec.	Marries Mary Cyrene Burch. Father of six children.
1844	Opens Law office in Georgetown, Kentucky.
1845	Moves to Lexington.
1847	Major, 3d Kentucky Volunteers, Mexican War.
1849	Elected to Kentucky State Legislature.
1851	Elected to Congress. First of two terms.
1853	Declines Governorship of Washington Territory.
1854	Accepts challenge to duel with New York Congressman Cutting.
1855	Declines appointment as Minister to Spain. Refuses to run for Congress.
1856	Elected Vice President of the United States, age 36 years.

1859, Dec.	Elected to the United States Senate for term beginning Mar. 4, 1861.
1860, Mar. 28	Receives the 33d° Ancient Accepted Scottish Rite, Southern Jurisdiction.
1860	Presidential nominee of Southern Faction (State Rights), Democratic Party. Receives 72 Electoral Votes.
1861, Mar. 4	Sworn in as Senator by Hannibal Hamlin, whom he had sworn in as Senator in 1857.
1861, Sep.	Resigns from the U.S. Senate.
1861, Nov.	Appointed Brigadier General, Confederate Army. Destined to serve as subordinate commander in six major battles and campaigns.
1861, Dec. 2	Declared a traitor by U.S. Senate.
1862	Promoted to Major General, Confederate States Army.
1864	Hero of the Battle of New Market, Virginia.
1865, Feb. 4	Appointed Secretary of War by Jefferson Davis.
1865, July 7	Embarks for Europe to avoid capture by Federal Troops.
1866	Sees victorious Prussian Troops in Berlin following their seven week war with Austria.
1867	Travels through Europe, Holy Land, and Egypt.
1868, Mar.	Has audience with Pope Pius IX in Rome.
1868, June 4	Sails for Canada.
1869, Mar. 9	By amnesty granted by President Johnson Dec. 25, 1868, returns to Kentucky.
1870	Denounces the Ku Klux Klan.
1875, May 14	Visited during final illness by Vice President Henry Wilson.
1875, May 17	Expires at his home in Lexington following abdominal operation. Age 54. Kentucky Legislature Resolution: "We leave the impartial

judgment of history to place him among the actors of his time as his talents and the services may entitle him, feeling no apprehension that posterity will not deprecate or underestimate the exalted virtues we knew him to possess.''

1887   Life-sized statue near courthouse in Lexington, Kentucky erected in his honor.

1969   Kentucky Historical Highway Marker states: "CAMP BRECKINRIDGE Army post built in 1942, on 36,000 acres, at cost of $39,000,000. Named for John C. Breckinridge, U.S. Vice President, 1856–60*; Confederate Secretary of War, 1865. Created as infantry training center for up to 40,000 men. Used during World War II, 1943–46, as prisoner of war camp for as many as 3,000 enlisted men of German Army." The Marker is #1424.

*Term was 1857-1861

Courtesy of Lexington Cemetery. Photograph by Ruth W. Laird

Lexington Cemetery. Kentucky Historical Highway Marker.

At the Lexington Cemetery entrance, 833 West Main Street, Lexington, Kentucky stands a Kentucky Historical Highway Marker. The inscription reads:

LEXINGTON CEMETERY
INCORPORATED IN 1849. LEXINGTON
CEMETERY WAS LAID OUT AS A NATURAL
LANDSCAPE PARK. BOTH CONFEDERATE
AND UNION SOLDIERS ARE BURIED
IN THIS CEMETERY. TOWERING OVER
HENRY CLAY'S GRAVE IS A 120-FOOT
MONUMENT SURMOUNTED BY HIS STATUE.
OTHER NOTED MEN, INCLUDING JAMES
LANE ALLEN, JOHN C. BRECKINRIDGE,
AND JOHN H. MORGAN, INTERRED HERE.
Presented by Lexington-Fayette
Co. Historical Commission.

Beside the statue on the Courthouse grounds in Lexington is a Kentucky Historical Highway Marker which reads:

U.S. VICE PRESIDENT

———————

JOHN CABELL BRECKINRIDGE, 1821–75
ONE OF FOUR KENTUCKIANS — MORE
THAN ANY STATE, EXCEPT NEW YORK —
WHO WERE U.S. VICE PRESIDENTS.
OTHERS WERE ADLAI E. STEVENSON,
RICHARD M. JOHNSON, AND ALBEN W.
BARKLEY. IN THE U.S. CONGRESS, 1851–55
ELECTED VICE PRESIDENT in 1856
CANDIDATE OF THE SOUTHERN DEMOCRATS
FOR PRESIDENT IN 1860. CARRYING
NINE SOUTHERN STATES. See over.
VICE PRESIDENT, CONT.

Photos by Robert F. Wachs.

Vice President and Mrs. John Cabell Breckinridge Monuments

Burial Plot in the Lexington Cemetery. Six Generations of the Breckinridge Family.

BRECKINRIDGE SERVED AS A MAJOR OF
KENTUCKY VOLUNTEERS, MEXICAN WAR.
ELECTED TO U.S. SENATE IN 1860.
BECAME BRIG. GENERAL, CONFEDERATE
ARMY, 1861, AND WAS EXPELLED FROM
THE SENATE. IN BATTLES OF SHILOH,
CHATTANOOGA, MURFREESBORO, AND
OTHERS. CONFEDERATE SECRETARY OF
WAR, FEB. 1865 UNTIL SURRENDER OF
LEE AT APPOMATTOX, APRIL 1865. HE
WAS BORN AND DIED IN LEXINGTON.

The eight-foot high statue of Breckinridge on the Courthouse grounds at Cheapside Street is supported by a four-foot, eight-inch high, four-foot square pedestal, resting on a base three feet high and fifty-two inches square. The foundation consists of three steps, each eight inches high, twelve feet square at the bottom, nine feet square in the middle, and eight feet square at the top.

The inscription on the pedestal reads:

JOHN CABELL
BRECKINRIDGE

ERECTED BY
THE COMMONWEALTH
OF
KENTUCKY
AD 1887

The monument marking the grave of John Cabell Breckinridge is located in the Breckinridge burial plot north of section C near the grave of Henry Clay in the Lexington Cemetery. The scroll-shaped marble stands forty-two and one half inches high and is twenty-two inches wide. The top of the scroll is five inches in diameter, and the bottom nine inches. Viewed

Robert F. Wachs Photographs

Ruth W. Laird Photograph

Vice President J. C. Breckinridge's descendents were military officers in the twentieth century.

Photo by Ruth W. Laird

Photo by Ruth W. Laird

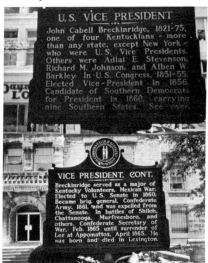

Kentucky historical highway marker #741 honoring Vice President

John Cabell Breckinridge statue, Court House grounds, Lexington, KY

from the side, the slab appears to be an unrolled scroll. The inscription, in one and three fourths-inch high letters, reads:

JOHN C. BRECKINRIDGE
BORN JAN. 16th 1821
DIED MAY 12th 1875

As one faces the Vice President's monument, a similar one to the right marks the grave of Mrs. Breckinridge. It reads:

MARY C. BRECKINRIDGE
WIFE OF
JOHN C. BRECKINRIDGE
BORN AUG. 16th 1826
DIED OCT. 8th 1907

Farther to the right is a stone marking the grave of the Vice President's father. It has the following inscription:

JOSEPH CABELL BRECKINRIDGE
BORN JULY 24, 1788
DIED SEPT. 1, 1823
"The righteous shall be in everlasting Remembrance" Adams

To the left of the Vice President's grave is that of a son, marked by a stone one foot wide and one and one half feet high. The inscription reads:

JOHN CABELL
INFANT SON AND
FOURTH CHILD
OF
JOHN C. AND MARY C.
BRECKINRIDGE

Ruth W. Laird Photograph.

Arkansas State Society, D.A.R. Memorial

The large Celtic Cross marks the grave of the great-grandson of the Vice President. The inscription on the base in front reads:

JOHN CABELL BRECKINRIDGE
1st LT. U.S. MARINES
1925–1951
KILLED IN ACTION
KOREA

The rear reads:

Beloved Son of
James C. and Dorothy T.
Breckinridge
Loved Brother of
JAMES THOMPSON BRECKINRIDGE

The D.A.R. flag holder at the monument of Katherine Carson, wife of Clifton R. Breckinridge, was placed by the D.A.R. in 1970:

ORGANIZING REGENT AND FIRST STATE REGENT
ARKANSAS STATE SOCIETY, D.A.R.

(15)   HANNIBAL HAMLIN
March 4, 1861 — March 3, 1865

(Lincoln — First Term)

Courtesy of Library of Congress.

Hannibal Hamlin statue in U.S. Capitol "Hall of Fame."

1809, Aug. 27	Born at Paris Hill, Maine.
1822	Finishes early education at Paris Hill School.
1826	Is graduated from Hebron Academy.
1828	Begins teaching school at Paris Hill; joins Hampden Rifles.
1832	Studies Law in Law office of Fessenden & Deblois, Portland, Maine.
1833, Dec. 10	Marries Sarah Jane Emery. Father of four children.
	Admitted to the Bar and opens office in Hampden, Maine.
1835	Captain, Hampden Rifles.
1836	Maine Legislator.
1837, Sep. 13	Third son born. Speaker, Maine House of Representatives.
1842	Elected to U.S. Congress.
1848	Elected to U.S. Senate.
1854	Votes against repeal of Missouri Compromise.
1855, Apr. 17	First wife passes away.
1856, Sep. 25	Marries Ellen Vesta Emery. Father of two children. Elected Governor of Maine.
1857	Resigns as Governor and is appointed U.S. Senator.
1858	Is hailed as Father of the Republican Party.
1860	Enlists as Private in Co. A, Maine Coast Guard; elected Vice President.
1861, Jan. 17	Resigns from Senate; sworn in as Vice President March 4th.
1862, Jan.	Advises President Lincoln to relieve General McClellan as Military Commander.

1864	Serves period of active duty with Maine State Guard at Kittery, thus qualifies for membership in GAR; is not selected to succeed himself as Vice Presidential nominee; praises candidate selected as "faithful among the faithless."
1865	Appointed Collector of the Port of Boston.
1866	Resigns as Collector of the Port of Boston.
1867	Publicly calls for the impeachment of President Johnson.
1869	Elected U.S. Senator.
1879	Last speech in Senate is in opposition to restriction of Chinese Immigration.
1881	Appointed Minister to Spain.
1887	Recommends that Lincoln's birthday be declared a National holiday.
1891, Feb. 12	In Lincoln Day speech in New York City repeats his plea that Lincoln's birthday be made a National holiday.
1891, July 4	Passes away while playing cards at the Tarratine Club, Bangor, Maine, at age of 81 years.
1935	Bronze Statue placed in Statuary Hall of the U.S. Capitol to represent Maine. The statue is six feet, eight inches tall and signed top base "Charles E. Tefft, 1933." The citation: HANNIBAL HAMLIN, 1809-1891, MAINE Statesman, U.S. House of Representatives 1843-47; U.S. Senate 1848-57, and resigned to become Governor of Maine 1857. Reelected to the U.S. Senate 1857-61; elected Vice President under Lincoln 1861-65. Enlisted as a private in the Maine State Guard, Civil War 1864; collector of port of Boston; U.S. Senate 1869-81; U.S. Minister to Spain 1881-82, when he resigned to devote the remainder of his life to agricultural pursuits.

Photographs by Joanne Monaghan

Headstone of Vice President Hamlin

Hannibal Hamlin burial plot cenotaph and headstones of Vice President Hamlin and his second wife.

The grave of Hannibal Hamlin, fifteenth Vice President of the United States, is located in Lot #3 in the Mount Hope Cemetery, Bangor, Maine. It is situated between Riverside and Front Avenues. Entrance is made by steps located in the center of the lot's west border, which measures thirty-one feet. Frontage on the avenues is twenty-six feet.

In the center of the plot is a cenotaph whose long axis is parallel with Riverside and Front Avenues. It is shaped like a sarcophagus with a base seven feet long, five and one half feet wide, and nine inches high. The coffin-shaped crown is sixty-eight inches long, twenty-six inches wide, and thirty-six inches high. The side facing north has this inscription in four-inch high letters:

HANNIBAL HAMLIN

The south side reads:

HANNIBAL HAMLIN
1809–1891

All of the granite headstones in the plot have the same shape. Each base is eight inches wide and twenty-two inches long. Each crown is twelve and one half inches long, eight inches high, and two and one half inches thick.

Eight graves are located along the north border and the inscriptions on each headstone face north.

Burials, from east to west, along the northern border include:

Grave Number	Name	Not on Stone	Dates
1	Sarah J. Hamlin	Daughter	1847–1878
2	Sarah J. Hamlin	First Wife	1815–1855
3	George E. Hamlin	Son	1835–1844
4	George E. Hamlin	Son	1848–1849
5	Cyrus Hamlin	Son, Civil War General	1839–1867
6	Ellen V. Hamlin	Second Wife	1835–1925
7	Hannibal Hamlin	15th Vice President	1809–1891
8	Frank Hamlin	Son	1862–1922

MOUNT HOPE CEMETERY
HAMLIN PLAT OF BURIALS

SOUTH

RIVERSIDE AVENUE FRONTAGE 26 FEET

16	15	14	13	12	11	10	9

EAST

FRONTAGE

31 FEET

HAMLIN CENTOAPH

18

STEPS

WEST

FRONTAGE

31 FEET

1	2	3	4	5	6	7	8

26 FEET

FRONT STREET FRONTAGE

NORTH

Grave number 18, located just south of Vice President Hamlin's grave between the entrance steps and the west end of the cenotaph, is that of Hannibal Emery Hamlin, 1858–1938, the first child of Hannibal and Ellen Vesta Emery.

Charles Hamlin, 1837–1911, a Civil War General, and the last surviving child of Hannibal and Sarah Jane Emery, is buried in grave number 16, south.

Nowhere in the Hamlin plot is there an inscription indicating that Hannibal Hamlin had been the fifteenth Vice President of the United States.

His headstone has the inscription:

1809
HANNIBAL HAMLIN
1891

Metal G A R flag holders are located at the headstones of Vice President Hamlin and his sons Cyrus and Charles.

(15 Conf.)   ALEXANDER HAMILTON STEPHENS
February 9, 1861 — May 11, 1865

(Davis)

Vice President of the Confederate States of America
Declared a traitor 1861.
Granted amnesty 1868.

Photographs by Patricia Lee Carter. Georgia Department of Natural Resources Division of Parks and Historic Sites

Alexander Hamilton Stephens Statue at grave site

Alexander Hamilton Stephens   Chronology
Vice President of the Confederacy
(Jefferson Davis, President of the Confederacy)

1812, Feb. 11	Born near Crawfordville, Wilkes County, Georgia.
1826	Enrolled in Locust Grove School.
1827	Enrolled in Washington Academy; adds Hamilton to his name because of his admiration for the principal, Alexander Hamilton Webster.
1832	Is graduated from the University of Georgia. Roommate of Crawford W. Long, first Doctor of Medicine to use anesthetic in a surgical operation (1842), in Jefferson, Georgia.
1833	Begins reading Law in Crawfordville.
1834	Admitted to the Bar.
1836	State Representative until 1842.
1842	Georgia State Senator.
1843	Enters U.S. House of Representatives, serving until 1859.
1848	Involved in an affray with Judge Francis N. Cone.
1856	Challenges Benjamin Harvey Hill to a duel.
1861	Vice President of the Confederate States.
1863	Heads mission to discuss prisoner exchange.
1865 May–Oct.	Imprisoned in Fort Warren, Boston.
1866	Elected to the U.S. Senate, but excluded by vote of Senate.
1867	Begins to write *The Constitutional History of the Late War Between the States*.

1869	Declines offer to become Professor of Political Science at the University of Georgia.
1871	Writes *School History of the United States.*
1872	Publishes *The Atlanta Sun.*
1873	Defeated in a race for the U.S. Senate, but is elected Congressman, and serves until 1882.
1882	Resigns as Congressman and is elected Governor of Georgia.
1883, Mar. 4	Expires in Governor's Mansion, Atlanta, Georgia and is interred in the Oakland Cemetery, Atlanta. Age 71 years.
1884	Reinterred in the front lawn of his home, Liberty Hall, Crawfordville, Georgia.
1893, May	Life-sized statue unveiled at grave site.
1913, Oct. 19	Memorial ledger over grave dedicated.
1927	Marble statue placed in Statuary Hall in the U.S. Capitol to represent Georgia.* The statue, seated, is five feet eight inches tall, and was executed by Gutzon Borglum, 1926–27. The citation: "ALEXANDER HAMILTON STEPHENS, 1812–1883, GEORGIA. Lawyer, U.S. Representative 1843–59; elected to the Confederate Congress and chosen vice president of the provisional government of the Confederacy, 1861–65; was elected to the U.S. Senate after the war but was denied admission; author of the War Between the States; U.S. House of Representatives, 1873–82; Governor of Georgia, 1882–83."
1931	Bronze statue of his contemporary President of the Confederacy, Jefferson Davis, placed in Statuary Hall to represent Mississippi.**

1932   Liberty Hall deeded to the State of Georgia and now administered by the Department of Natural Resources, Division of Parks and Historic Sites.

*Dr. Crawford W. Long, roommate of Alexander H. Stephens at the University of Georgia, had his marble statue unveiled in the National Statuary Hall Collection in 1926. The sculptor was J. Massey Rhind; the statue is located in the Senate connecting corridor. Dr. Long also represents the State of Georgia. The citation reads:

"Dr Crawford Williamson Long, 1815–1878, Georgia. Physician, humanitarian; first surgeon to use sulphuric ether as an anesthesia in 1842, considered one of the great events in the history of surgery."

The 7'2" marble statue was executed by J. Massey Rhind, 1924–25.

**A bronze statue of Stephens' contemporary President, Jefferson (Finis) Davis stands in the rotunda of the Kentucky State Capitol in Frankfort, Kentucky. The citation on the pedestal has this inscription:

JEFFERSON DAVIS
BORN FAIRVIEW, KENTUCKY JUNE 3, 1808
DIED DECEMBER 6, 1889
ONLY PRESIDENT OF THE CONFEDERACY
PATRIOT   HERO   STATESMAN
JUNE 3, 1808–DECEMBER 6, 1889
TRANSYLVANIA UNIVERSITY 1821–1824
WEST POINT 1824–1828
BLACK HAWK WAR 1833
U.S. HOUSE OF REPRESENTATIVES 1845–1846
MEXICAN WAR 1847
U.S. SENATE 1845–1853
SECRETARY OF WAR 1853–1857
U.S. SENATE 1857–1861
PRESIDENT CONFEDERATE STATES OF AMERICA
1861–1865

Courtesy of the Alexander H. Stephens Memorial.
Photograph by Ruth W. Laird

Alexander H. Stephens statue viewed from the South

The citation on the base of the bronze statue of Jefferson Davis contemporary President of the Confederacy reads:

"Jefferson Davis, 1808–1889, Mississippi. Soldier, statesman, President of the Confederacy. A graduate of West Point; fought in the Black Hawk War, 1830–31; the War with Mexico. As Secretary of War under President Pierce 1853–57 he had jurisdiction over the erection of the new House and Senate wings and the dome of the U.S. Capitol. U.S. House of Representatives 1845–46; U.S. Senator 1847–51, 1857–61. Elected President of the Southern Confederacy 1862.*"

*Term began February 18, 1861 in Montgomery, Alabama.

The 7'7" bronze statue was executed by Augustus Lukeman in 1928.

Carl Schurz said of him: "I was struck by the dignity of his bearing, the grace of his diction, and the rare charm of his voice."

The monument marking the grave of Alexander Hamilton Stephens is located in the front lawn of his plantation, Liberty Hall, Crawfordville, Georgia.

It is twenty feet high, including the life-sized statue of the Confederate Vice President. The statue faces south.

Three step-like stones, roughly eight, six, and four feet square and a total of three feet high, support a ten-foot high and three-foot square pedestal with four faces. A civic wreath and crossed quills cover the top front and symbolize his greatness as a statesman, historian, and author. Each of the other sides is embellished by a trefoil cross and other designs. The south face reads:

BORN FEB. 11, 1812
MEMBER GA. HOUSE OF REPRESENTATIVES
1836 TO 1840
MEMBER GA. STATE SENATE 1842
MEMBER U.S. HOUSE OF REPRESENTATIVES
1843 TO 1859
RETIRED FROM CONGRESS 1859
VICE PRESIDENT CONFEDERATE STATES
1861 TO 1865
U.S. SENATOR ELECT FROM GEORGIA, 1866
MEMBER U.S. HOUSE OF REPRESENTATIVES
1873 TO 1882
GOVERNOR OF GEORGIA 1882.
DIED IN ATLANTA, GA.,
SUNDAY MORNING MARCH 4, 1883

AUTHOR OF "A CONSTITUTIONAL
VIEW OF THE WAR
BETWEEN THE STATES" AND
A COMPENDIUM OF THE HISTORY
OF THE UNITED STATES FROM
THEIR EARLIEST SETTLEMENT
TO 1872.

Courtesy of Library of Congress.

Alexander Hamilton Stephens statue in U.S. Capitol "Hall of Fame."

Ruth W. Laird Photographs

East Face of Monument Inscription

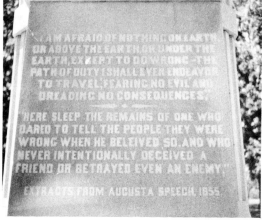

West Face of Monument Inscription

North Face of Monument Inscription

South Face of Monument Inscription

ALEXANDER H. STEPHENS in four-inch high letters is carved on the top step of the supporting pedestal.

The east face inscription reads:

THROUGHOUT LIFE A SUFFERER IN BODY,
MIND, AND SPIRIT, HE WAS A SIGNAL
EXAMPLAR OF WISDOM, COURAGE, FORTITUDE,
PATIENCE, AND UNWEARYING CHARITY.
IN THE DECREPITUDE OF AGE, CALLED TO
BE GOVERNOR OF THE STATE. HE DIED,
WHILE IN PERFORMANCE OF THE WORK
OF HIS OFFICE, AND IT SEEMED FIT,
THAT HAVING SURVIVED PARENTS,
BRETHREN, SISTERS, AND MOST OF
THE DEAR COMPANIONS OF YOUTH,
HE SHOULD LAY HIS DYING HEAD
UPON THE BOSOM OF HIS PEOPLE.

The graves of Alexander Hamilton Stephens and his half brother Linton Stephens are located in a plot surrounded by a field stone wall sixteen feet long, fourteen feet wide, and three feet high. It is just east of the Vice President's statue.

Outside the stone enclosure, located at the northwest corner, is a granite stone, two feet by one foot in size and flush with the turf, with an arrow pointing south which says "To Street" and another arrow pointing east which says "To Eliza Stephens' property."

The large inscription on the stone reads:

PROPERTY OF ESTATE
OF
ALEXANDER H. STEPHENS

The memorial ledger covering the grave of Alexander Hamilton Stephens consists of a white marble slab six and one half feet long, three and one half feet wide, and six inches thick. It is supported by a marble base seven feet six inches long by four feet six inches wide.

The head of the ledger is toward the east.
It is ornamented by the seal of the Gate City Guard.
The inscription reads:

Photograph by Patricia Lee Carter. Georgia Department of Natural Resources Division of Parks and Historic sites

Alexander Hamilton Stephens Memorial Ledger

THIS TABLET
IS A TRIBUTE FROM THE
OLD GUARD
OF THE
GATE CITY GUARD
TO THE MEMORY OF THEIR
DEPARTED FRIEND
ALEXANDER HAMILTON STEPHENS
PATRIOT AND STATESMAN
VICE PRESIDENT
OF THE
CONFEDERATE STATES OF AMERICA
BORN FEBRUARY ELEVENTH 1812
DIED MARCH FOURTH 1883
HIS REMAINS REST BENEATH THIS TABLET

———————*———————

DEDICATED OCTOBER NINETEENTH 1913

South of the seal of the Gate City Guard is a marble slab, two feet by one foot in size, flush with the turf, with this inscription:

LINTON STEPHENS
GEORGIA
LT. COL. 15 REGT GA INFANTRY
CONFEDERATE STATES ARMY
JULY 1, 1823   JULY 14, 1872

The west face is inscribed:

"I AM AFRAID OF NOTHING ON EARTH
OR ABOVE EARTH, OR UNDER THE
EARTH, EXCEPT TO DO WRONG — THE
PATH OF DUTY I SHALL EVER ENDEAVOR
TO TRAVEL, FEARING NO EVIL AND
DREADING NO CONSEQUENCES."

Photograph by Patricia Lee Carter. Georgia Department of Natural Resources Division of Parks and Historic Sites

Linton Stephens Headstone

Ruth W. Laird Photograph.

Liberty Hall Inscription

"HERE SLEEP THE REMAINS OF ONE WHO
DARED TO TELL THE PEOPLE THEY WERE
WRONG WHEN HE BELIEVED SO, AND WHO
NEVER INTENTIONALLY DECEIVED A
FRIEND OR BETRAYED EVEN AN ENEMY."
EXTRACTS FROM AUGUSTA SPEECH, 1855.

The north face reads as follows:

THE GREAT COMMONER
THE DEFENDER OF
CIVIL AND RELIGIOUS LIBERTY
"HE COVETED NOR TOOK FROM THE
REPUBLIC NOTHING SAVE GLORY."

NON SIBI, SED ALUS

A bronze plaque attached to a large field stone stands at the road beside the walk leading to Alexander H. Stephens' former home, Liberty Hall. The inscription reads:

LIBERTY HALL
HOME OF
ALEXANDER HAMILTON STEPHENS
1845–1883
PROPERTY DEEDED BY
EXECUTORS TO STEPHENS MONUMENTAL
ASSOCIATION JUNE 4, 1885 — TO STATE
OF GEORGIA, DECEMBER 31, 1932.
BUILDING DEDICATED JULY 18, 1935.
WPA   1936   UDC

(16)   ANDREW JOHNSON
March 4, 1865 — April 15, 1865

(Lincoln — Second Term)

Succeeded to the Presidency upon death of Lincoln

Courtesy of Andrew Johnson Historic Site

Andrew Johnson Grave Monument

Andrew Johnson   Chronology   Sixteenth Vice President
          (Lincoln   Second Term)

1808, Dec. 29	Born in Raleigh, North Carolina.
1822	Apprenticed to a tailor.
1824	Runs away from his apprenticeship.
1826	Moves to Tennessee and soon opens his own tailor shop in Greeneville.
1827, May 17	Marries Eliza McArdle. Father of five children.
1829	Elected Alderman.
1830	Mayor of Greeneville. Acquires own building for tailor shop.*
1831	Trustee of Rhea Academy.
1835	State Legislator.
1838	Purchases home across street from tailor shop.
1839	State Legislator.
1841	State Senator.
1842	Elected to U.S. Congress.
1843	Begins first of five terms as Congressman.
1851, Sep.	Purchases an eight room brick house on Main Street.
1851	Becomes a Master Mason, Greeneville Lodge #119, F&AM.
1853	Governor of Tennessee: Establishes State Department of Agriculture; initiates appropriations for public schools; fosters "Grange".
1857	U.S. Senator.
1860, Dec. 19, 20	Opposes secession in memorable Senate speeches.

1862	Military Governor of Tennessee with rank of Brigadier General.
1864	Elected Vice President of the United States.
1865, Apr. 15	Succeeds to Presidency upon death of Lincoln.
1866	Enforces the Monroe Doctrine against French in Mexico.
1867	Approves Alaska Purchase.
1868, Feb. 24	House of Representatives votes for his impeachment.
1868, May 16, 26	Senate vote on impeachment: NOT GUILTY.
1868, Dec. 25	Issues Amnesty Proclamation for all who had been in secession (rebellion against the Federal Government).
1869	Returns to Greeneville and fails to win seat in U.S. Senate.
1872	Fails to win seat in House of Representatives.
1874	Elected to the U.S. Senate.
1875	Sworn in as Senator by Vice President Henry Wilson, who, as Massachusetts Senator, had voted YES in his impeachment trial. Johnson offers him his hand, and Wilson takes it, amidst thunderous applause; meets thirteen other Senators, eleven of whom had voted to impeach.
1875, July 31	Dies at Carter Station, Tennessee at the age of 66 years.
1906	Johnson Cemetery becomes Federal property.
1921	State of Tennessee purchases tailor shop and encloses it in a brick building.
1926	U.S. Supreme Court rules that Tenure of Office Act is unconstitutional.
1935	Act of Congress makes Johnson Cemetery and Tailor Shop a National Monument.

1941	Federal Government purchases his last home.
1962	State of Kentucky Historical Highway Marker located in Ft. Thomas, Kentucky notes that Henry Stanbery, U.S. Attorney General in 1866, resigned in 1868 to become legal counsel for President Johnson in his impeachment trial. After the trial, Johnson reappointed him Attorney General, but the Senate refused to confirm the appointment.
1963	Cemetery, tailor shop, and last residence designated a National Historic Site under the administration of the U.S. Department of Interior.
1970	U.S. Department of Interior develops plans to restore the first home Johnson owned, across College (Water) Street from the tailor shop.

The monument marking the grave of Andrew Johnson, the sixteenth Vice President of the United States, is located in the Andrew Johnson National Cemetery, Greeneville, Tennessee. Now known as Monument Hill, it originally consisted of fifteen acres, owned by Andrew Johnson. It is now part of the Andrew Johnson National Historic Site, administered by the National Park Service of the Department of the Interior.

*Andrew Johnson's tailor shop dates its existence as such from 1830 until 1843. The wooden building is about eighteen feet long and fourteen feet wide. It stands on its original site at the Visitor's Center of the Andrew Johnson National Historic Site at the corner of Depot and College Streets, Greeneville, Tennessee. It was enclosed in a brick building in 1921.

The monument is a marble shaft twenty-five feet in height. It is adorned by an American eagle, poised for flight.

Beneath the feet of the eagle and draping the upper third of the shaft is a carving of the flag of the Republic.

Near the base of the shaft is a scroll-like carving on which is written:

CONSTITUTION
OF THE
UNITED STATES

Just beneath the scroll is an open Bible, upon the right side of which is superimposed the sculpture of a hand. This symbolizes his placing his hand on the Bible and taking the oath to defend the Constitution.

Flanking the scroll and the Bible are two torches. The torch on the monument's right is plain, while the other is ornamented with handles.

The base of the monument bears these inscriptions:

ANDREW JOHNSON
SEVENTEENTH PRESIDENT
OF THE UNITED STATES
BORN DEC. 29, 1808
DIED JULY 31, 1875

HIS FAITH IN THE PEOPLE NEVER WAVERED

ELIZA JOHNSON
BORN OCT. 4, 1810
DIED JAN. 19, 1876
IN MEMORY OF OUR
FATHER AND MOTHER

The burial plot is surrounded by an iron picket fence.

Photo Courtesy of Tim Frazier, Staff Photographer, Tenn. Dept. of Conservation.

Johnson Tailor Shop as it appears in the brick building built by the state of Tennessee in 1921.

Courtesy of Tennessee Conservation Department

Andrew Johnson Tailor Shop as it appeared prior to 1921.

(17)   SCHUYLER COLFAX
March 4, 1869 — March 3, 1873

(Grant — First Term)

Michael Wright Photo. Northern Indiana Historical Society, South Bend.

Schuyler Colfax Monument

Schuyler Colfax   Chronology   Seventeenth Vice President
                     (Grant   First Term)

1823, Mar. 23	Born in New York City.
1836	Moves to New Castle, Indiana.
1841	Moves to South Bend, Indiana.
1842	Begins informal study of Law.
1844, Oct. 10	Marries Evelyn E. Clark.
1845	Owner and editor of Whig newspaper.
1846	Joins the Independent Order of Odd Fellows.
1851	Writes the Degree of Rebekah.
1855	Elected to Congress.
1856	Becomes a Master Mason in St. Joseph Lodge #54, F&AM, South Bend, Indiana.
1863	Elected Speaker of the House of Representatives, serves until 1869.
1868, July 10	First wife passes away.
1868, Nov. 18	Marries Ellen W. Wade. Father of one son.
1868	Votes YES on House resolution to impeach President Johnson.
1869	Receives Honorary LLB Degree from Indiana University.
	Inaugurated Vice President under Grant, first term.
1870	Announces retirement from political life. Son born.
1873	Receives Honorary LLB Degree from Otterbein College. Is threatened with impeachment because of alleged "Credit Mobilier" involvement. Joins the Chautauqua lecture circuit.
1876	"Abraham Lincoln" speech widely acclaimed.

1883   "Landmarks of Life" speech published in the *Congregationalist* magazine.

1885, Jan. 13   Passes away in Mankato, Minnesota at the age of 61 years.

1937, Oct. 31   American Legion Post #50 of South Bend dedicates plaque beside his grave in the Old City Cemetery which notes that he was Vice President of the United States 1869–1873.

1978, May 13   Odd Fellows and Rebekahs of Indiana dedicate commemorative plaque at his grave in the Old City Cemetery, South Bend, Indiana.

Courtesy of Old City Cemetery. Robert C. Niezgodski Photo

Odd Fellows & Rebekah Memorial.

In the Old City Cemetery, 214 Elm Street, at the end of Colfax Avenue, South Bend, Indiana a six-foot high by seventeen-inch square white marble monument marks the grave of Schuyler Colfax. It faces east and has four-inch high letters on the base which read:

COLFAX

The pedestal carries the following inscription completely enclosed by braces:

SCHUYLER COLFAX
DIED
JAN. 13, 1885
AGED 61 YEARS

Just north of this monument is a two-foot by one-foot granite stone with this legend:

SCHUYLER COLFAX
HERE LIES THE AUTHOR OF THE
DEGREE OF REBEKAH, WRITTEN IN 1851.
DEDICATED BY THE ODD FELLOWS AND
REBEKAHS OF INDIANA.
MAY 13, 1978

Odd Fellow and Rebekah symbols flank the top of the memorial. Besides the Rebekah stone is a bronze plaque which reads:

SCHUYLER COLFAX
VICE PRESIDENT OF THE UNITED STATES
1869 TO 1873
STATESMAN AND BELOVED CITIZEN
SOUTH BEND POST 50 AMERICAN LEGION
ACKNOWLEDGES THE SERVICES
HE RENDERED HIS COUNTRY

The north side of the monument records the following:

EVELYN E.
WIFE OF
SCHUYLER COLFAX
DIED
JULY 10, 1868
AGE 40 Years
"The path of the just is as
a shining light that shineth more
and more unto the perfect day"
Proverbs 4:18

On the west side:

ELLEN WADE COLFAX
WIFE OF
SCHUYLER COLFAX
DIED MARCH 4, 1911
AGE 74 YEARS

On the south side:

SCHUYLER COLFAX, JR.
APRIL 11, 1870
MARCH 29, 1925

On the west border of the twenty-seven by twelve-foot plot are seven headstones.

The twin stones to the south have "Catherine" and "Ellen" carved on the top, while the face of each records, right to left:

ELLEN NELSON COLFAX
Born June 1, 1901
Died Oct. 6, 1904

CATHERINE SCHUYLER COLFAX
Born August 20, 1902
Died October 7, 1904
"Of such is the Kingdom of Heaven"

Courtesy of Old City Cemetery. Robert C. Niezgodski Photo

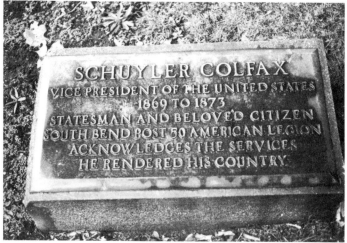

American Legion Memorial.

Michael Wright Photo.

Colfax Inscription.

To the left of the twin stones, on the top rim:

CNC

On the face:

CATHERINE NELSON
COLFAX
WIFE OF
SCHUYLER COLFAX, JR.
Born Feb. 7, 1871
Died July 29, 1955

The remaining stones carry no inscriptions.

Courtesy of Old City Cemetery. Ruth W. Laird Photo.

Daughter-in-Law Monument.

(18)   HENRY WILSON
March 4, 1873 — November 22, 1875

(Grant — Second Term)

Died in office

Courtesy of Old Dell Park Cemetery. Photograph by Ruth W. Laird

Grave of Henry Wilson

Henry Wilson   Chronology   Eighteenth Vice President
                     (Grant   Second Term)

1812, Feb. 16	Born at Farmington, New Hampshire; named Jeremiah Jones Colbath.
1822	Indentured to farmer.
1833	Indenture ends; moves to Massachusetts and has name changed by Act of Legislature to Henry Wilson.
1834	Apprentice shoemaker in Natick, Massachusetts.
1834	After three months as apprentice, buys out of apprenticeship. Joins Massachusetts Militia (National Guard).
1836	On visit to Washington, DC sees slave pens and auction blocks that makes him anti-slavery
1837	Attends Strafford, Wolfborough, and Concord Academies.
1838	Helps form Natick Debating Society to oppose slavery. Manufactures shoes.
1839	Defeated in try for seat in State Assembly.
1840, Oct. 28	Marries Harriet Malvina Howe. Father of one son. Earns title of Natick Cobbler. Elected to Massachusetts House of Representatives.
1844	Elected to Massachusetts Senate.
1845	Opposes annexation of Texas.
1846, Nov. 11	Only child is born.
1848	Defeated in attempt to fill Congressional seat of John Quincy Adams; edits *Boston Republican*.
1851	President of Massachusetts Senate.

1852	Brigadier General, State Militia; fails in try for office of Governor of Massachusetts.
1854	Joins American "Know Nothing" Party.
1855, Feb. 10	Elected to U.S. Senate as replacement for Edward Everett.
1856	Denounces American Party; declines duel challenge by Preston Brooks.
1859	Begins second term in United States Senate.
1861	Chairman of Senate Committee on Military Affairs.
1865	Begins third term as United States Senator. Author *Anti-Slavery Measures of the 37th and 38th Congresses.*
1866	Author *Military Measures of the United States Congress.*
1866, Dec. 24	Only son dies while serving with Northern Occupation Forces in Texas.
1867	Author *Testimonies of American Statesmen and Jurists to the Truths of Christianity.*
1868, May 16, 26	Votes YES to impeach President Johnson. Author "History of Reconstruction Measures of the 39th and 40th Congresses."
1870, May 28	Wife passes away.
1871, June	Takes first extended vacation; visits London, Berlin, Vienna.
1872	Elected Vice President of the United States.
1873, May 19	Suffers paralysis of face muscles.
1874	Receives Honorary LLD Degree from Dartmouth College.
1875, Mar.	Swears in Andrew Johnson as Senator from Tennessee. During the impeachment trial, Wilson had called him a violator of the Constitution, a violator of the Laws, a violator of his oath. When Johnson offers him his hand in unfeigned cordiality, Wilson takes it, amidst thunderous applause.

1875, May 14	Visits former Vice President John C. Breckinridge, who is terminally ill, in Lexington, Kentucky.
	Author *History of the Rise and Fall of Slave Power in America.*
1875, Nov. 22	Expires in Vice President's room in Capital at the age of 63.
1902	A bronze plaque is placed on the wall near his bust in the formal office of the Vice President (S 214) in the Senate wing, second floor of the US Capitol. The 10½ x 14½ plaque reads:

IN THIS ROOM
HENRY WILSON
VICE PRESIDENT OF
THE UNITED STATES
AND A SENATOR
FOR EIGHTEEN YEARS
DIED NOVEMBER 22, 1875
THE SON OF A FARM LABORER.
NEVER AT SCHOOL MORE THAN
TWELVE MONTHS. IN YOUTH A
JOURNEYMAN SHOEMAKER,
HE RAISED HIMSELF TO
THE HIGH PLACES OF
FAME, HONOR and POWER,
AND BY UNWEARIED STUDY
MADE HIMSELF AN
AUTHORITY IN THE HISTORY OF
HIS COUNTRY AND OF LIBERTY
AND AN ELOQUENT
PUBLIC SPEAKER TO WHOM
SENATE AND PEOPLE
EAGERLY LISTENED.
HE DEALT WITH AND
CONTROLLED VAST
PUBLIC EXPENDITURE DURING A
GREAT CIVIL WAR,
YET LIVED AND
DIED POOR, AND LEFT TO HIS
GRATEFUL COUNTRYMEN THE
MEMORY OF AN
HONORABLE PUBLIC SERVICE,
AND A GOOD NAME
FAR BETTER THAN RICHES.

1970   Oil portrait painting By Darius Cobb
                       placed in the Mary Ann Morse Institute
                       Library, Natick, Massachusetts.
                       The accompanying citation reads:
                       Henry Wilson   February 16, 1812 —
                                    November 22, 1875
                             Vice-President of the United States
                                    1873–1875
                             Buried in Old Dell Park Cemetery,
                                    Natick, Mass.
                       Elected Representative from Natick to
                       General Court of Massachusetts 1840.
                       Elected to Massachusetts State Senate
                       1844.
                       Elected to United States Senate 1855.
                       Chairman of Committee on Military
                       Affairs during the Civil War.
                       Brigadier General Massachusetts Militia.
                       "To Henry Wilson Equal Rights were not
                       idle words"
1978   "Henry Wilson was an eloquent leader in
                       every Congressional step taken for the
                       benefit of the black race."

The monument marking the grave of Henry Wilson is located in the Old Dell Park Cemetery, Natick, Massachusetts.

The burial plot is demarcated by four fourteen-foot long,
eight-inch wide, and one-foot, eight-inch high solid slabs of
grey granite. It has six corner markers of granite, each one foot
square, and one foot ten inches high. The mound is reached by
two four-foot wide steps. The entire plot measures twelve yards
by nine yards.

The plot is dominated by a white marble monument erected
in 1867 in memory of the Wilson's only child, Henry Hamilton
Wilson. The coffin-shaped memorial is fifty-seven inches long,
twenty-one inches wide, and twenty-seven inches high. It rests
on a granite base sixty-one inches long, twenty-six inches wide,
and nine inches high.

Courtesy of Old Dell Park Cemetery. Ruth W. Laird Photograph

LTC Henry Hamilton Wilson Grave Monument

Courtesy of Old Dell Park Cemetery. Ruth W. Laird Photograph

Mary Tombs Howe Grave Monument

It is surmounted by a hat, feather, sword, belt, and sash.
The front bears this inscription:

LIEUT. COLONEL
HENRY HAMILTON WILSON
BORN IN NATICK
NOV. 11, 1846
DIED AT AUSTIN, TEXAS
DEC. 24, 1866
ARMY OF THE POTOMAC

The rear carries:

"HE THE YOUNG AND STRONG, WHO CHERISHED
NOBLE LONGINGS FOR THE STRIFE,
BY THE ROAD-SIDE FELL AND PERISHED
WEARY WITH THE MARCH OF LIFE"
DEP. OF THE SOUTH — DEP. OF THE GULF

A GAR flag holder stands beside the monument.

Courtesy of Old Dell Park Cemetery. Ruth W. Laird Photograph

Mrs. Henry Wilson Grave Monument

Six feet behind this monument is a headstone, small, coffin-shaped, one foot eight inches long, ten inches wide and eleven inches high, with this inscription:

HAMILTON

In line with the headstone of Wilson's son and to the far left of it is a white marble, coffin-shaped monument thirty-one inches long, fourteen inches wide, and twenty inches high, surmounted by an open Bible where the ribbon on the left side reads:

HOLY BIBLE

The monument inscription reads:

MARY TOMBS
WIDOW OF AMASA HOWE
BORN IN HOPKINTON, MASS.
SEPT. 11, 1786
DIED AUG. 27, 1881

"GOD IS LOVE"

To the right of the son's headstone is a white marble monument, similar in size to that of Mary Tombs, with a sprig of lily on top. The inscription reads:

HARRIET M. HOWE
BORN IN NATICK, NOV. 21, 1824
MARRIED TO HENRY WILSON, OCT. 28, 1840
DIED MAY 28, 1870
SHE MADE HOME HAPPY

The base of the monument carries this sentiment:

"BUT O FOR THE TOUCH OF A VANISHED HAND
AND THE SOUND OF A VOICE THAT IS STILL".

To the right of this monument, as one faces it, is a coffin-shaped marble memorial twenty-four inches long, ten inches wide, fourteen inches high, and seven inches thick, which bears this inscription:

HENRY WILSON

A metal GAR flag holder stands between the graves of Mrs. Wilson and her husband.

To the right of Henry Wilson's grave are those of his father and mother, marked by twin marble upright slabs thirty-one inches high, nineteen inches wide, four inches thick, supported on a common base and foundation.

The one on the left is inscribed:

ABIGAIL COLBATH
BORN MARCH 21, 1785
DIED AUG. 8, 1866

The one on the right:

WINTHROP COLBATH
BORN APRIL 7, 1787
DIED FEB. 10, 1860

Courtesy of Old Dell Park Cemetery.

Abigail & Winthrop Colbath Grave Monument

In Jonathan B. Mann's book entitled *The Life of Henry Wilson,* published in 1872, the following inscription was mentioned as appearing on the monument of Henry Wilson:

"NO MONUMENT A BROADER BASE SUSTAINS
THAN THINE MUST HAVE — ON EQUAL RIGHTS AND LAWS:
NO MEMORY THE CONTINENT RETAINS
TRUER TO GOD'S WILL AND MANHOOD'S HOLY CAUSE."

It could not be located at the burial plot nor otherwise substantiated.

Photograph by Ruth W. Laird

Henry Wilson Cobbler's Shop.

Two miles west of the center of the town of Natick, the eighteen by twelve-foot building used by Henry Wilson carries a plaque above the front window which states:

IN THIS LITTLE SHOP
HENRY WILSON
20th VICE PRESIDENT OF THE UNITED STATES*
LEARNED TO MAKE SHOES
WAS KNOWN AS THE NATICK COBBLER

*Was the 18th Vice President of the United States.

(19)   WILLIAM ALMON WHEELER
March 5, 1877 — March 3, 1881

(Hays)

Courtesy of Morningside Cemetery. Ruth W. Laird Photograph

William Almon Wheeler Monument.

William Almon Wheeler   Chronology
Nineteenth Vice President
(Hays)

1819, June 30	Born at Malone, New York
1838	Is graduated from Franklin Academy, Malone's high school.
1839	Country school teacher.
1840	Awarded diploma by the University of Vermont.
	Becomes Town Clerk and studies Law.
1845	Opens Law office in Malone
1845, Sep. 17	Marries Mary King.
	Appointed School Commissioner and School Inspector of Malone Public Schools.
1847	Elected Franklin County District Attorney.
1850–51	Banker and State Assemblyman. Ways & Means Committee Chairman.
1853–66	Northern Railroad mortgage holder trustee.
1857	Elected New York State Senator
1858–60	President Pro-Tempore New York State Senate.
1861–63	Representative in the United States Congress.
1867–68	President of the New York State Constitutional Convention.
1869	Representative in Congress.
1873	Vigorously opposes "Salary Grab" Act.
1873	Speaker of the House of Representatives for brief time.
1875	Chairman of the House Committee on Southern Affairs.

1876, Mar. 3	Wife passes away at the age of 48 years.
1876, Dec.	Advances Wheeler Adjustment to settle election dispute in Louisiana.
1877, Mar. 3	Elected Vice President by one electoral vote.
1879	Settles factional dispute among sections of the New York Republican Party.
1881	Declines to be a candidate for the United States Senate.
1887, June 4	Passes away at his home in Malone, New York at the age of 67 years.
1930	Former home on Elm Street, Malone, New York acquired by the Malone Lodge of Elks.
1932	A New York State Education Historical Marker, erected in front of his Elm Street home, states:

HOME OF
WILLIAM ALMON WHEELER
1819–1887; ATTORNEY, BANKER,
ASSEMBLYMAN, STATE SENATOR,
CONGRESSMAN, VICE-PRESIDENT
OF UNITED STATES 1877–81.

1977, Mar. 4	One Hundredth Anniversary Ceremonial is held in his former home, 67 Elm Street, Malone, New York, commemorating his inauguration as Vice President of the United States.
1977, June 30	Elvira Hosson's oil painting of Vice President Wheeler is presented to the Franklin County Historical and Museum Society of Malone, New York.

The grave of William Almon Wheeler, nineteenth Vice President of the United States, is located in the Morningside Cemetery, Malone, New York.

Photographs by Robideau Studios, Malone, New York

Elm Street House—last home of Vice President Wheeler

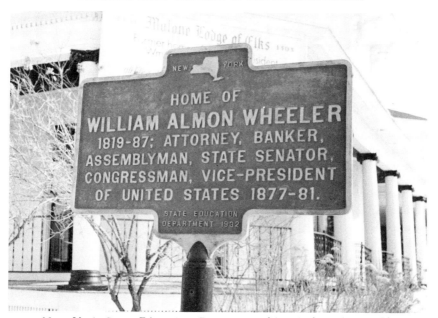

New York State Education Department historical marker at Elm Street home of Vice President Wheeler

The Wheeler-King burial plot is forty feet long and twenty-four feet wide. It is demarcated by a granite wall fifteen inches high. Two-foot six-inch high granite posts are located in the wall at the corners of the plot, at the entrance steps, and midway along the sides and rear of the enclosure. The front of the left half of the plot as one faces it has "WHEELER" inscribed in four-inch high letters, while the right half has the name "KING".

The Vice President's grave monument stands in the center of the Wheeler plot. The crown of the monument is a white marble slab sixty-six inches high, thirty-two inches wide, and twelve inches thick. On the thirty-eight-inch wide, fourteen-inch high base is the word:

WHEELER

in five-inch high letters. The entire monument is supported by a granite foundation forty-five inches by twenty-six inches by eleven inches high. The inscription reads:

WILLIAM A. WHEELER
BORN JUNE 30, 1819
WAS THUS HONORED:
MEMBER OF N.Y. LEGISLATURE.
REP. IN CONGRESS FIVE TERMS.
PRES. OF N.Y. CONS. CON 1867.
VICE-PRES. U.S. 1876–80*
DIED JUNE 4, 1887
A FAITHFUL PUBLIC SERVANT

*Term was 1877–1881

Courtesy of Morningside Cemetery. Ruth W. Laird Photograph

Wheeler Burial Plot Monuments.

Courtesy of Morningside Cemetery. Ruth W. Laird Photograph

Jane M. and Fidelia Wheeler Grave Monuments

As one faces the Vice President's monument, to the right is a white marble slab fifty-two inches high which reads:

MARY KING
WIFE OF
WM. A. WHEELER
DIED MARCH 3, 1876
IN THE 49th YEAR OF
HER AGE

———————

A DEVOTED WIFE

Above the inscription is a laurel wreath which surrounds an intricately designed monogram using the letters "WAW" and "MK."

To the left of the William A. Wheeler stone is a monument similar in size, shape, and design for Almon and Eliza Wheeler, parents of the Vice President. The epitaph on the base reads:

TAKE THEM O FATHER IF YOU MUST
ASHES TO ASHES AND DUST TO DUST
TILL THE LAST ANGEL ROLLS THE STONE AWAY
AND A NEW MORNING BRINGS ETERNAL DAY.

The two memorial slabs to the rear of the Wheeler plot mark the graves of Jane M. and Fidelia Wheeler, sisters of William Almon Wheeler.

(20)   CHESTER ALAN ARTHUR
March 4, 1881 — September 19, 1881

(Garfield)

Succeeded to the Presidency upon death of Garfield

Courtesy of Albany Rural Cemetery.

Sarcophagus of Chester Alan Arthur.

Chester Alan Arthur   Chronology   Twentieth Vice President
(Garfield)

1830, Oct. 5	Born at Fairfield, Vermont.
1848	Is graduated from Union College and elected to Phi Beta Kappa.
1850	Begins study of Law; national president of Psi Upsilon.
1851	Principal, North Pownal, Vermont Academy.
1853	Completes legal training in New York City.
1854	Admitted to the New York City Bar.
1855	Wins suit that leads to integration of city street cars.
1857	Judge Advocate of New York Militia.
1859, Oct. 25	Marries Ellen Lewis Herndon. Father of three children.
1861	Brigadier General, Engineer Corps, State Militia.
1862	Quartermaster General, New York State Militia.
1863	Resumes private practice of Law.
1871	Appointed Collector of the Port of New York by President Grant.
1878	Declared by President Hays to be incompetent and is summarily relieved as Port Collector.
1880, Jan. 12	Wife passes away. Elected Vice President.
1881, Sep. 20	Succeeds to the Presidency; backs civil service reform.
1882	Vetoes Chinese Exclusion Act; signs Treaty of Peace with Korea.
1884	Fails to win nomination for Presidency.
1885	Resumes private practice of Law.

1886, Nov. 18   Passes away at age of 56 years.

1899   Full length bronze statue unveiled on northeast corner of small park at Madison Square, New York City.

The monument marking the grave of Chester Alan Arthur, twentieth Vice President of the United States, is located in the Albany Rural Cemetery, Menands-Watervliet, New York.

The burial plot is approached by five white granite steps. Each copestone of the walls of the steps is ornamented by a bronze urn.

With the Napoleon sarcophagus for its motif, the memorial has excellent proportions, and its plain and highly polished dark Quincy granite makes it impressive. A feeling of *Awe and Inspiration* is elicited by the bronze Angel of Bereavement standing by the pedestal at the head of the sarcophagus. Her left hand, palm up, extends along the four-sided roof and is placing on the tomb the palm branch of victory and peace. This last symbolic earthly tribute sweeps over the foot of the memorial and bends gracefully downward over the end.

The angel's right arm hangs extended by her side, with her hand touching one of the bronze wings.

On the front of the base, between the supporting black granite pedestals of the sarcophagus, is the word:

ARTHUR

A bronze plaque, attached to the top of the base just in front of the rear pedestal, bears this inscription:

CHESTER ALAN ARTHUR
21st PRESIDENT OF THE UNITED STATES
BORN, OCTOBER 5, 1830; DIED, NOVEMBER 18, 1886

Courtesy of Art Commission of the City of New York.

Chester Alan Arthur Statue, Madison Square, New York City.

Behind the sarcophagus is a seven-foot by one and one half-foot rectangular white granite stone. Superimposed thereon is the sword and cross of a crusader. Around the border is this inscription:

"Here lies the Body of Ellen Lewis Herndon, Wife of
CHESTER ALAN ARTHUR
Born at Culpeper, C. H., Virginia, August 30, 1837. Died at
New York, Jan. 12, AD 1880"

An adjoining stone reads:

Chester Alan Arthur II, Son of Chester Alan Arthur &
Ellen Lewis Herndon
Born at New York City July 25, 1864
Rowena Dashwood, Second wife of Chester Alan Arthur II
Born at Colorado Springs November 8, 1894
Died at Colorado Springs November 5, 1965
Chester Alan Arthur III, son of Chester Alan Arthur II &
Myra Townsend Fithian, born at Colorado Springs
March 21, 1901

The pedestal of the Chester A. Arthur statue located near Madison Square in New York City has this inscription:

CHESTER ALAN
ARTHUR
TWENTY-FIRST PRESIDENT
OF
THE UNITED STATES
OF AMERICA

(21)   THOMAS ANDREWS HENDRICKS
March 4, 1885 — November 25, 1885

(Cleveland — First Term)

Died in office

Courtesy of Crown Hill Cemetery.

Thomas A. Hendricks Monument

Thomas Andrews Hendricks   Chronology
Twenty-First Vice President
(Grover Cleveland   First Term)

1819, Sep. 7	Born at Zanesville, Ohio.
1837	Is graduated from Greensburg Academy.
1841	Is graduated from Hanover College, Hanover, Indiana.
1843	Begins study of Law in Chambersburg, Law Department of Gettysburg College.
1845	Opens Law office; marries Eliza Morgan. Father of one son.
1848	Member, State of Indiana Legislature.
1851	Begins two terms as Congressman.
1854	Votes for repeal of Missouri Compromise.
1855	Commissioner of United States Land Office.
1860	Defeated for office of Governor of Indiana.
1863	Elected to the U.S. Senate.
1865	Opposes 13, 14, 15th Amendments to the U.S. Constitution.
1868, May 16, 26	Votes NOT GUILTY in impeachment trial of President Andrew Johnson. Defeated for office of Governor.
1872	Receives 42 electoral votes for the Presidency.
1873–1877	Governor of Indiana.
1877, Mar. 3	Fails to become Vice President of the United States by one electoral vote.
1880	Has first paralytic stroke.
1885, Mar. 4	Vice President of the United States.

1885, Nov. 25   Passes away in Indianapolis, Indiana at age of 66 years, the fourth Vice President to die in office. At this time there is no line of succession for the Presidency, since the Special Session of Congress adjourned without electing a House Speaker or a President Pro-Tempore of the Senate.

The burial plot of Vice President Hendricks is located in section twenty-nine of the Crown Hill Cemetery, Indianapolis, Indiana.

A beautifully carved, four-sided shaft of granite ten feet long, supported by a four-foot square, five-foot high pedestal, marks his grave. On the base of the pedestal, front and rear, in five-inch high letters, is the following:

T. A. HENDRICKS

Side by side and west of the obelisk, at turf level, are two stones twelve inches by eighteen inches in size. The one to the north has the initials:

E.C.H.

The one to the south:

T.A.H.

A similar stone on the south, in three-inch high letters reads:

MORGAN

The shield of the west side of the monument, in two-inch high letters, has this inscription:

THOMAS A.
HENDRICKS
BORN SEPTEMBER 7, 1819
DIED NOVEMBER 25, 1885

ELIZA C.
HENDRICKS
BORN NOVEMBER 23, 1823
DIED NOVEMBER 3, 1903

The shield on the south is inscribed:

MORGAN
SON OF
THOMAS AND ELIZA
HENDRICKS
BORN AT SHELBYVILLE, IND.
JANUARY 16, 1848
DIED MARCH 10, 1851

A State of Indiana Historical Marker located at the administrative office of the Crown Hill Cemetery reads:

CROWN HILL CEMETERY, FOUNDED IN 1863, IS
THE FOURTH LARGEST CEMETERY IN AMERICA.
THE HISTORY OF INDIANA AND THE UNITED STATES
IS REFLECTED IN ITS MONUMENTS. PRESIDENT
BENJAMIN HARRISON, VICE PRESIDENTS CHARLES
FAIRBANKS, THOMAS HENDRICKS,
AND THOMAS MARSHALL,
INNOVATORS RICHARD GATLING
AND COL. ELI LILLY,
AUTHOR BOOTH TARKINGTON AND POET JAMES
WHITCOMB RILEY ARE AMONG THE MANY
POLITICAL, COMMERCIAL AND LITERARY
LEADERS BURIED WITHIN
ITS BOUNDS. CROWN HILL IS THE ONLY CEMETERY
IN THE STATE LISTED ON THE NATIONAL REGISTER
OF HISTORIC PLACES.

Courtesy of Crown Hill Cemetery. Ruth W. Laird Photograph

Hendricks Monument Inscription.

Courtesy of Crown Hill Cemetery. Ruth W. Laird Photograph

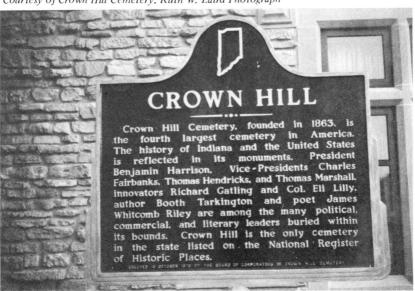

Crown Hill Historical Marker.

(22) LEVI PARSONS MORTON
March 4, 1889 — March 3, 1893

(Benjamin Harrison)

Courtesy of Rhinebeck Cemetery. Ruth W. Laird Photograph

LEVI PARSONS MORTON
1824 — 1920
A · SERVANT · OF · THE · NATION
—
Member · of · Congress
Minister · to · France
Governor · of · New · York
Vice · President · of · the · United · States

MORTON

Morton Cenotaph.

Levi Parsons Morton   Chronology
        Twenty-Second Vice President

(Benjamin Harrison)

1824, May 16	Born at Shoreham, Vermont
1843	Without formal education, becomes store manager.
1845	Cotton merchant, Hanover, New York.
1849	Cotton merchant, Boston, Massachusetts.
1854	Merchantile executive, New York City.
1855	Importer and wholesaler; entrepreneur.
1856, Oct. 15	Marries Lucy Young Kimball. Father of one daughter.
1861	Business fails.
1863	Launches banking firm in New York City; repays creditors.
1869	International Banker.
1871, July 11	First wife passes away.
1873, Feb. 12	Marries Anna Livingston. Father of five daughters and one son.
1879	Member of the U.S. House of Representatives
1881	Minister to France.
1884	Accepts Statue of Liberty from the French Government on behalf of the United States.
1885	Presents a replica of the Statue of Liberty to the citizens of France for display in Paris. Cattle breeder and farmer. Defeated in try for the United States Senate.
1886, Oct.	Guest of Honor as President Cleveland accepts the Statue of Liberty and dedicates Liberty Island in New York Harbor.

1887	Defeated in second try for a seat in the United States Senate.
1888	Elected Vice President under Benjamin Harrison.
1889, Mar. 4	Vice President of the United States.
1895	Governor of New York.
1897	Returns to banking.
1899	Launches Morton Trust Company.
1909	Forms the Guaranty Trust Company of New York.
1911, Apr. 19	Signs pledge to finance the completion of the choir of the Cathedral Church of St. John the Divine in New York City.
1918, Aug. 14	Second wife passes away at the age of 72 years.
1920, May 16	Expires at his home in Rhinecliff, New York, at the age of 96 years.
1922	In the south gateway of the ambulatory leading around the choir of the Cathedral Church of St. John the Divine, a white marble tablet bearing this inscription is dedicated:

TO THE GLORY OF GOD AND IN ENDURING MEMORY OF LEVI PARSONS MORTON, 1824–1920, VICE PRESIDENT OF THE UNITED STATES, GOVERNOR OF THE STATE OF NEW YORK, AND OF HIS WIFE, ANNA LIVINGSTON MORTON, 1846–1918, WHOSE GIFTS MADE POSSIBLE THE BUILDING AND THE FURNISHING OF THE CHOIR OF THIS CATHEDRAL. YEA SAID THE SPIRIT, THAT THEY MAY REST FROM THEIR LABOURS, AND THEIR WORKS DO FOLLOW THEM. |

The sixteen-yard square Morton burial plot is located in the southwest corner of the Rhinebeck Cemetery, Rhinebeck, New York. The cemetery is one and one half miles south of the Beekman Arms Hotel, the oldest hotel in America, on New York route 9.

The plot is demarcated by an iron pipe boundary twenty-four inches high, and completely hidden by a hedge of yew shrubs over six feet high.

Nine flat slabs of white granite mark the burial sites. Those of the adults measure seventy inches long by thirty-seven inches wide. Those of the children, forty-two inches long by nineteen inches wide.

The south end of each memorial ledger is ornamented by a Latin cross encircled by laurel. The cross on the adult ledger is eight inches wide by thirteen inches long; on that of the children, four inches wide and six and one half inches long.

The memorial ledger marking the grave of Levi Parsons Morton is number one in the plat and bears this inscription:

LEVI PARSONS MORTON
BORN MAY 16, 1824
DIED MAY 16, 1920

THE PATH OF THE JUST IS AS A SHINING LIGHT
THAT SHINETH MORE AND MORE UNTO
THE PERFECT DAY.

His grave is flanked by those of his first wife, Lucy, and his second wife, Anna, numbers two and eleven in the plat diagram.

Number Two
LUCY KIMBALL
WIFE OF
LEVI P. MORTON
DIED IN NEWPORT, R.I.
JULY 11, 1871
AGE 34 YR.

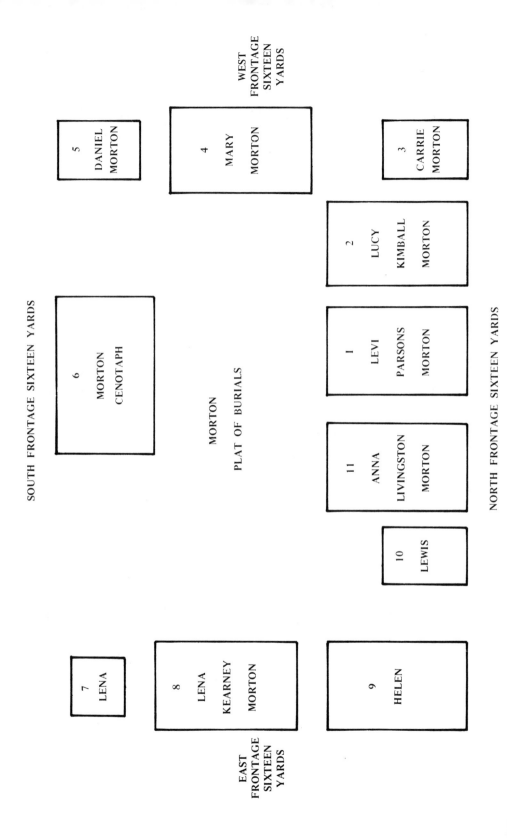

SOUTH FRONTAGE SIXTEEN YARDS

WEST FRONTAGE SIXTEEN YARDS

NORTH FRONTAGE SIXTEEN YARDS

EAST FRONTAGE SIXTEEN YARDS

MORTON

PLAT OF BURIALS

5
DANIEL
MORTON

4
MARY
MORTON

3
CARRIE
MORTON

2
LUCY
KIMBALL
MORTON

6
MORTON
CENOTAPH

1
LEVI
PARSONS
MORTON

11
ANNA
LIVINGSTON
MORTON

10
LEWIS

7
LENA

8
LENA
KEARNEY
MORTON

9
HELEN

Number Three
CARRIE
INFANT DAUGHTER OF
LEVI P. AND LUCY K.
MORTON
DIED JULY 3, 1857

Number Four
MARY MORTON
DAUGHTER OF
LEVI P. MORTON AND
ANNA LIVINGSTON MORTON
BORN JUNE 10, 1881
DIED IN SWITZERLAND
APRIL 20, 1932

FIGHTING THE GOOD FIGHT OF FAITH
LAYING HOLD ON ETERNAL LIFE

Number Five
DANIEL O. MORTON
DIED DEC. 6, 1862
AGED 5 YEARS
& 11 MOS.

Number Six
CENOTAPH

The Cenotaph has a foundation from east to west seventy-eight inches long and forty-eight inches wide. The base is seventy inches long, forty inches wide and twelve inches high. The front of the base, facing north, has this inscription in four-inch high letters:

MORTON

The sixty-inch long, thirty-inch wide, and twenty-inch high crown carries the following:

LEVI PARSONS MORTON
1824–1920
A SERVANT OF THE NATION
MEMBER OF CONGRESS
MINISTER TO FRANCE
GOVERNOR OF NEW YORK
VICE-PRESIDENT OF THE UNITED STATES

The east end carries the following:

ANNA LIVINGSTON   1846–1918
WIFE OF LEVI P. MORTON
THEIR CHILDREN
LEWIS PARSONS MORTON   1877–1878
LENA KEARNY MORTON   1875–1905
MARY MORTON   1881–1932
HELEN MORTON   1876–1952

The west face carries the following:

LUCY KIMBALL   1836–1871
WIFE OF LEVI P. MORTON
THEIR DAUGHTER
CARRIE MORTON   1857–1857

DANIEL O. MORTON   1857–1862
SON OF
DANIEL O. AND ELIZABETH TYLER MORTON

The eight-inch high cap is ornamented with a Celtic cross, with the arms of the cross to the west and east.

Number seven

Courtesy of Rhinebeck Cemetery. Photograph by Ruth W. Laird

Cenotaph. East End

Courtesy of Rhinebeck Cemetery. Photograph by Ruth W. Laird

Cenotaph. West Face

This monument is a white marble Calvary cross forty-nine inches vertically and twenty-eight inches horizontally. It rests on a three-step-like base. The top step is thirteen and one half inches square and the middle step is twenty-two and one half inches square, and they carry the following:

IN THY PRESENCE
IS FULLNESS OF JOY
LENA MORTON
1875–1904

Number Eight
LENA KEARNEY MORTON
DAUGHTER OF
LEVI P. MORTON AND
ANNA LIVINGSTON MORTON
DIED IN PARIS, FRANCE
JUNE 10, 1905*
AGE 29 YEARS
HER TONGUE WAS THE LAW OF KINDNESS

Number Nine
HELEN MORTON
BORN AUGUST 2, 1876
DIED SEPTEMBER 6, 1952
IN THE HEAVENLY KINGDOM IS
THE DWELLING OF THY SAINTS
AND THEIR REST IS FOR EVERMORE

*Date body was returned from France.

Courtesy of Rhinebeck Cemetery.
Ruth W. Laird Photograph

Lena Morton Monument.

Number Ten
LEWIS PARSONS
SON OF L. P. MORTON
AND
ANNA LIVINGSTON
MORTON
DIED IN LONDON
JANUARY 20, 1878

COME UNTO ME

Number Eleven
ANNA LIVINGSTON MORTON
BORN MAY 18, 1846
DIED AUGUST 14, 1918
I WILL LIFT UP MINE EYES UNTO THE
HILLS FROM WHENCE COMETH MY HELP

I, **Levi Parsons Morton**, of the Parish of Grace Church in the City of New York, having with the blessing of **Divine Providence**, been permitted to provide means for the completion of the **Choir** of the

Cathedral Church of Saint John the Divine

in the City and Diocese of New York, including the Altar, Reredos, Organ and Choir Stalls, do hereby ask the Trustees of the said Cathedral to accept these Memorial Gifts, which are offered to the

Glory of God

and in recognition of the great value of the said Cathedral to the Church at large, to this Diocese and to this Community; and to accept them as the fulfillment of my pledge to cooperate with them in completing the **Choir**, and making it ready for its consecration.

In Witness Whereof, I have hereunto set my hand this nineteenth day of April in the year of our **Lord** one thousand nine hundred and eleven.

Levi Parsons Morton

Morton pledge to complete choir of Cathedral Church of St. John the Divine in New York City.

(23)   ADLAI EWING STEVENSON
March 4, 1893 — March 3, 1897

(Cleveland — Second Term)

Photos by Robert E. Handley.

Stevenson Monument. (Front)

Adlai Ewing Stevenson   Chronology
Twenty-Third Vice president

(Cleveland — Second Term)

1835, Oct. 23	Born near Herndon, Christian County, Kentucky.
1852	Student, Illinois Wesleyan University.
1854	Teaches country school and begins study of Law.
1857	Admitted to the Bar in Bloomington, Illinois.
1858	Opens Law office in Metamora, Illinois.
1861	Organizes 108th Illinois Militia Regiment. Master-in-Chancery, Woodford Circuit Court; State's Attorney.
1866	Withdraws as student in Centre College, Danville, Kentucky.
1866, Dec. 20	Marries Letitia Green of Danville. Father of four children.
1869	Becomes a Master Mason in Bloomington Lodge #43, F&AM.
1874, Jan. 1	Elected Worshipful Master of Lodge #43, F&AM.
1874, Nov.	Elected to first term in Congress.
1877	Board of Visitors, West Point.
1878	Chairman of Committee on Mines and Mining.
1885	Appointed First Assistant Postmaster General.
1889	Appointment to U.S. Supreme Court not confirmed.
1892	Elected Vice President of the United States.
1897	Appointed head of Bimetallic Monetary Commission.

1900	Candidate for Vice President on Bryan ticket.
1908	Defeated in race for office of Governor of Illinois.
1909	Author of *Something of Men I Have Known*.
1913, Dec. 25	Wife passes away.
1914, June 14	Expires in Chicago at the age of 78 years.
1952	Grandson Adlai Ewing Stevenson defeated in race for the office of President of the United States.
1956	Grandson again unsuccessful in race for the Presidency.
1962	Kentucky Historical Highway Marker on Route 117 near Herndon reads: "Adlai Ewing Stevenson, 1835-1914, one of four Kentuckians — more than any State, except New York — who were U.S. Vice Presidents. Others were Richard M. Johnson, John C. Breckinridge and Alben W. Barkley.
	Stevenson, born here, moved to Illinois, 1852.
	Member of Congress two terms. Elected Vice President with Cleveland in 1892. Bryan's running mate in 1900."
1973	First article on his political career by L. C. Schlup appears.
1976–77	Three articles on his political career by Leonard Clarence Schlup published.

The monument marking the grave of Adlai Ewing Stevenson is located in the Evergreen Memorial Cemetery, Bloomington, Illinois.

The base is inscribed with:

STEVENSON — SCOTT

Robert E. Handley Photo

A. E. Stevenson Grave Monument. (Rear)

Beneath the laurel which ornaments the frieze of the massive granite stone are carved the following:

ADLAI EWING STEVENSON
VICE PRESIDENT OF THE UNITED STATES
Oct. 23, 1835 — June 14, 1914

LETITIA GREEN STEVENSON
HIS WIFE
Jany. 8, 1843 — Dec. 25, 1913

MATTHEW THOMPSON SCOTT
Feby. 24, 1828 — May 21, 1891

JULIA GREEN SCOTT
HIS WIFE
Feby. 14, 1839 — Apr. 29, 1928

The rear of the monument carries the following:

MARY E. STEVENSON
MARY HARDIN
LETITIA STEVENSON HARDIN
MAY 18, 1897 — JAN 28, 1920
LEWIS GREEN STEVENSON
AUGUST 15, 1888 — APRIL 5, 1929
HELEN DAVIS
HIS WIFE
SEPTEMBER 17, 1899 — NOVEMBER 18, 1923
MARTIN D. HARDON
June 5, 1873 — December 14, 1935
JULIA STEVENSON
HIS WIFE
June 30, 1874 — September 4, 1966
Adlai Ewing Stevenson
February 5, 1900 — July 14, 1965
Letitia Ewing Stevenson
June 22, 1876 — September 6, 1970
Ernest L. Ives
October 17, 1887 — March 4, 1972
Elizabeth Stevenson Ives
July 18, 1897 —

(24) GARRET AUGUSTUS HOBART
March 4, 1897 — November 21, 1899

(McKinley — First Term)

Died in office

Courtesy of Cedar Lawn Cemetery. Ruth W. Laird Photograph

Garret A. Hobart Mausoleum

Garret Augustus Hobart   Chronology
Twenty-Fourth Vice President
(William McKinley   First Term)

1844, June 3	Born at Long Branch, New Jersey.
1863	Is graduated from Rutgers College with highest honors.
1864	Teaches school and studies Law.
1866	Opens Law office in Paterson, New Jersey.
1869, July 21	Marries Jennie Tuttle. Father of two children.
1870	Becomes a Master Mason in the Falls City Lodge #82, F&AM, of Paterson, New Jersey.
1872	Elected to the State Assembly.
1874	Speaker of the House of Representatives of New Jersey.
1876	Elected New Jersey State Senator.
1881	Elected President of the New Jersey State Senate.
1884	Defeated in race for the U.S. Senate.
1885	Organizer, counselor, or director of sixty diverse corporations such as water, transportation, banking, manufacturing, utilities.
1896	Elected Vice President of the United States.
1899, Feb. 14	Casts deciding vote, thus denying Philippino independence, as provided in Bacon Amendment.
1899, Nov. 21	Passes away in Paterson, New Jersey at age of 55 years. The sixth Vice President to die in office.

1903, June 3   A nine-foot high bronze statue, on a nine-foot high pedestal, dedicated in front of the City Hall, Paterson, New Jersey. The inscription on the pedestal reads:

GARRET
AUGUSTUS
HOBART

The last resting place of Garret Augustus Hobart is located in the beautiful Cedar Lawn Cemetery, Paterson, New Jersey. His body is entombed in an impressive mausoleum thirty-eight feet long, nineteen feet wide, and twenty-two feet high. The exterior walls are of polished white granite. The four pillars are monoliths and rest on a three-step base. The entablature has a laurel wreath above each column.

Double open-work bronze doors, seven feet high and two and one half feet wide, permit a view of the white marble interior. Above the doors is the word HOBART.

In the rear wall above the sarcophagi is a leaded stained glass window of an ascending angel depicting the "Flight of the Soul".

Six feet from the left door is the white marble sarcophagus of Vice President Hobart which carries these words:

GARRET AUGUSTUS HOBART
1844–1899

Beside the sarcophagus of Mr. Hobart is that of his wife, whose inscription reads:

JENNIE TUTTLE
WIFE OF
GARRET A. HOBART
1849–1941

In a crypt to the right of the mausoleum entrance is the body of the daughter, Fannie Beckwith Hobart, who died in Italy June 27, 1895.

This imposing building was designed by Henry Bacon of New York City. It is technically known as Grecian Doric architecture. The stained glass window was executed by Louis Comfort Tiffany.

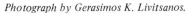

Photograph by Gerasimos K. Livitsanos.

Garret Augustus Hobart Statue, City Hall. Paterson, New Jersey.

Courtesy of Youngs Memorial Cemetery. Ruth W. Laird Photograph.

Theodore Roosevelt Admonition.

(25)   THEODORE ROOSEVELT
March 4, 1901 — September 14, 1901

(McKinley — Second Term)

Succeeded to the Presidency upon death of McKinley

Courtesy of Youngs Memorial Cemetery. Ruth W. Laird Photograph.

Theodore Roosevelt Grave Monument.

Theodore Roosevelt   Chronology
Twenty-Fifth Vice President
(McKinley   Second Term)

1858, Oct. 27	Born in New York City.
1864	Education begins with a series of private tutors.
1872	Obtains a collection of birds from Egypt and Palestine.
1880	Is graduated from Harvard. Earns Phi Beta Kappa Key.
1880, Oct. 27	Marries Alice Lee. Father of one daughter.
1881	Studies Law at Columbia University.
1882	New York State Assemblyman; serves until 1884.
1884, Feb. 14	First wife passes away at the age of 22 years.
1884	Rancher in North Dakota.
1886, Dec. 2	Marries Edith Kermit Carow. Father of five children. Defeated for the office of Mayor of New York.
1889	U.S. Civil Service Commission; serves until 1895.
1895	New York Board of Police Commissioners.
1897	Assistant Secretary of the Navy. Advises intervention in Cuba.
1898, May	Resigns Navy post and organizes Rough Rider Volunteers for the Spanish-American War. Commissioned Colonel.
1899	Governor of New York.
1900	Elected Vice President of the United States.
1901, Apr. 24	Becomes a Master Mason in Matinecock Lodge #806, F&AM, Oyster Bay, New York.

1901, Sep. 14	Succeeds to the Presidency.
1902	Intervenes in Venezuela. Pushes Spooner Act through Congress.
1903	Panama secedes from Columbia and is recognized as a nation.
1904, May 4	Work on the Panama Canal started by the United States.
1904, Nov. 8	Elected President of the United States.
1905	Intercedes as mediator in the settling of the Russo-Japanese War.
1906	Named to receive the Nobel Peace Prize.
1907	Sends the United States Fleet around the world.
1908	Creates the Conservation Commission to preserve the Nation's natural resources.
1909	Becomes contributing editor of the *Outlook* magazine.
1910–11	Conducts explorations in Africa for the Smithsonian Institution; tours Europe; travels to Christiana (Oslo) to receive Peace Prize.
1912	Organizes the Progressive Party and runs, unsuccessfully, for the Presidency.
1913–14	Leads exploration party to South America. Discovers a river which Brazil names Rio Teodoro.
1916	Denied command of a United States Military force.
1917	Author of *Foes of Our Own Household*.
1918	Author of *The Great Adventure; Present-Day Studies in American Nationalism*.
1919, Jan. 6	Passes away at his home at Sagamore Hill, Oyster Bay, New York. Age 60.
1922	Birthplace in New York City restored and open to the public.
1930	Theodore Roosevelt Island Memorial in the Potomac River established.

1933	New York State Theodore Roosevelt Memorial Building completed with an equestrian statue of Roosevelt in military uniform at the entrance, Central Park, New York City.
1935, April	Symbolic murals of his notable achievements unveiled in the Theodore Roosevelt Memorial Hall, New York City.
1939	Face unveiled on Mount Rushmore Shrine of Democracy Memorial, South Dakota.
1947	Theodore Roosevelt National Memorial Park established in North Dakota.
1950	Elected to the New York University Hall of Fame.
1954	Bust and tablet unveiled at the New York University Hall of Fame. Sculptor-Georg Lober: a gift of the Theodore Roosevelt Association.
1958	Birthplace at 28 East 20th Street, New York City becomes a National Historic Site.
1962	Kentucky Historical Highway Marker #699 states that "in 1904, Governor William O. Bradley, seconded nomination of Theodore Roosevelt."
1973	Sagamore Hill, home of Theodore Roosevelt, appears on the banner of the Oyster Bay Rotary Club.

The monument marking the grave of Theodore Roosevelt, the twenty-fifth Vice President of the United States, is located in plat #30 of the Youngs Memorial Cemetery, Oyster Bay, Long Island, New York.

The grey granite slab is sixty-nine inches high, thirty-seven inches wide, and seven and one half inches thick.

Six parallel grooves fifty-six inches long, supporting a six-inch square sculpture of a South American petunia, ornament each side of the slab.

Just beneath tne arch of the crown is a replica of the coat of arms of the office of President of the United States.

The inscription reads:

THEODORE ROOSEVELT
Born October 27, 1858
Died January 6, 1919
and his wife
EDITH KERMIT
Born August 6, 1861
Died September 30, 1948

As one views the monument through the twenty-one-foot square, eight-foot high iron fence enclosure, the grave of Theodore Roosevelt is on the left and that of Edith Kermit Roosevelt on the right.

Outside the enclosure, resting on the brick pavement, is a large boulder with a bronze plaque which has this inscription:

THEODORE ROOSEVELT
SAID
KEEP YOUR EYES ON THE STARS
KEEP YOUR FEET ON THE GROUND

(26)   CHARLES WARREN FAIRBANKS
March 4, 1905 — March 3, 1909

(Theodore Roosevelt — Second Term)

Courtesy of Crown Hill Cemetery.

CHARLES WARREN FAIRBANKS
U. S. SENATE 1897 — 1905
VICE PRESIDENT THE
UNITED STATES 1905 — 1909

CORNELIA COLE FAIRBANKS
PRESIDENT GENERAL
D.A.R.
1901 — 1905

FAIRBANKS

Fairbanks Plot Monument.

Charles Warren Fairbanks   Chronology
                 Twenty-Sixth Vice President
                 (T. Roosevelt   Second Term)

1852, May 11	Born in Unionville Center, Union County, Ohio.
1872	Is graduated with Bachelor of Arts Degree from Ohio Wesleyan University
1874, Oct. 6	Marries Cornelia Cole. Father of seven children.
	Admitted to the Bar, State of Ohio.
1875	Master of Arts, Ohio Wesleyan University.
1876	Opens Law office in Indianapolis, Indiana.
1893	Purchases the *Indianapolis News*.
1896	Elected to first of two terms in the U.S. Senate.
1904	Elected Vice President of the United States.
1904, Dec. 27	First Vice President to be made a Master Mason "at sight", Oriental Lodge #500, F & AM, Indianapolis, Indiana.
1905	First Vice President to become a Noble in the Mystic Shrine.
1913, Oct. 24	Wife passes away.
1916	Unsuccessful candidate for Vice President on ticket with Charles Evans Hughes.
1918, June 4	Expires in Indianapolis at age of 66 years.

The burial plot of Vice President Charles Warren Fairbanks is located in section twenty-four of the Crown Hill Cemetery, Indianapolis, Indiana.

An impressive granite memorial twelve feet high, six and one half feet wide, flanked by Ionic columns seven feet high, stands in front of the lot and faces north. The sculptured acanthus ornaments the roof.

The plot is forty-eight feet wide and one hundred five feet deep.

On the base of the monument, in five-inch high letters is the word:

FAIRBANKS

Courtesy of Crown Hill Cemetery. Ruth W. Laird Photograph

Fairbanks Monument Inscription.

The panel between the columns, in two-inch high letters, reads:

CHARLES WARREN FAIRBANKS
U.S. SENATE 1897 — 1905
Vice President the
UNITED STATES 1905 — 1909

CORNELIA COLE FAIRBANKS
PRESIDENT GENERAL
D.A.R.
1901 — 1905

Courtesy of Crown Hill Cemetery. Ruth W. Laird Photograph

Fairbanks Family Headstones.

To the rear of the plot monument are two rows of stones measuring one foot by two feet, flush with the turf. The row farthest to the rear consists of eight stones, each inscribed, respectively, from left to right:

Ethel Cassidy	Warren Charles	Charles Warren	Cornelia Cole
Fairbanks	Fairbanks	Fairbanks	Fairbanks
1882 — 1944	1878 — 1938	1852 — 1918	1852 — 1913
Louise Hubba	Frederick Cole	Richard Monroe	Robert F.
Fairbanks	Fairbanks	Fairbanks	Fairbanks
1889 — 1912	1881 — 1940	1884 — 1944	1886 — 1951

The row nearest the monument, from left to right:

Anne Albershort	Mary Adelaide	Mary Caperton
Fairbanks	Fairbanks	Fairbanks
1933 — 1963	1875 — 1961	1911 — 1967

(27)   JAMES SCHOOLCRAFT SHERMAN
March 4, 1909 — October 30, 1912

(Taft)

Died in Office

Photographs by Douglas M. Preston, Oneida Historical Society.

James Schoolcraft Sherman Mausoleum.

James Schoolcraft Sherman   Chronology
Twenty-Seventh Vice President
(William Howard Taft)

1855, Oct. 24	Born at Utica, New York.
1870	Attends Whitestown Seminary.
1878	Earns Bachelor of Arts Degree at Hamilton College.
1879	Earns LLB Degree at Hamilton College.
1880	Admitted to the Bar.
1881, Jan. 26	Marries Carrie Babcock. Father of three children.
1884	Mayor of Utica, New York.
1887	Begins first of two terms in Congress.
1893	Begins first of three additional terms in Congress.
1895	President of Hartford Canning Company.
1900	President of Utica Trust and Deposit Company.
1908	Elected Vice President of the United States.
1912	Renominated for office of Vice President on Republican ticket, the first Vice President to win a second nomination since Calhoun in 1828.
1912, Oct. 30	Expires in Utica at the age of 57 years, the seventh Vice President to die in office.
1923, July 21	Life-sized statue unveiled on Memorial Drive at Genesee Street, Utica, New York.

The grave of James Schoolcraft Sherman, twenty-seventh Vice President of the United States, is located in the Forest Hill Cemetery, Utica, New York.

His body lies in an unpolished, grey granite mausoleum twelve feet long, ten feet wide, and thirteen feet high. Crypts on either side, six feet eight inches long, add five feet eight inches to the width of the structure.

On either side of the entry are rough hewn Latin crosses whose vertical length is three feet two inches, and whose horizontal measurement is one foot ten inches. The bronze entrance doors are seven feet high and three feet two inches wide. The entablature above carries these words:

JAMES SCHOOLCRAFT SHERMAN

In the center, rear, of the mausoleum stands a double sarcophagus. In the front of the one on the left is this inscription:

JAMES SCHOOLCRAFT SHERMAN
VICE PRESIDENT OF THE UNITED STATES
BORN AT UTICA N.Y. OCTOBER 24, 1855
DIED AT UTICA N.Y. OCTOBER 30, 1912

On the top of the marble slab covering the sarcophagi is a Celtic cross whose center has a civic wreath. At the foot of the cross is the following:

OCT. 24, 1855   OCT. 30, 1912
JAMES SCHOOLCRAFT SHERMAN

The sarcophagus on the right has this inscription:

NOV. 16, 1856   OCT. 5, 1931
CARRIE BABCOCK

Courtesy of Forest Hill Cemetery. Ruth W. Laird Photograph

James Schoolcraft Sherman Mausoleum. (Front View)

A four-foot high by three-foot wide leaded stained glass window, translucent with the brilliant color of lilies, is in the rear wall of the mausoleum and carries this message:

"FOR SUCH IS
THE KINGDOM OF HEAVEN"

The middle crypt to the right of the entrance is inscribed:

SHERRIL SHERMAN
SON OF JAMES S. & CARRIE B. SHERMAN
MAY 1, 1883 — JUNE 1, 1962

The bottom crypt on the right:

BABY SHERMAN
MAR. 4, 1912
INFANT SON OF
SHERRIL & KATE BAKER SHERMAN
BABY WALDRON
MARK SHERRIL SON OF
JOHN & BARBARA SHERMAN
JAN. 2, 1964

The bottom crypt on the left:

COLONEL THOMAS MOORE SHERMAN
DEC. 24, 1885   FEB. 29, 1944

To the right of the approach walk near the mausoleum entrance is a two-foot by one-foot granite stone inscribed:

RICHARD UPDIKE SHERMAN
JULY 29, 1884 — DEC. 17, 1950

Courtesy of Forest Hill Cemetery. Ruth W. Laird Photograph

Richard Updyke Sherman Headstone.

Courtesy of Forest Hill Cemetery. Ruth W. Laird Photograph

Headstones of (left to right) Wm. B. Sherman, Kate B. Sherman, James
S. Sherman II.

A row of similar-sized stones is to the left of the entrance walk. The far left one is inscribed:

WILLIAM BAKER SHERMAN
JULY 26, 1917 — MAR. 27, 1948

The middle stone:

KATE BAKER SHERMAN
DEC. 22, 1877 — SEP. 5, 1960

The right stone:

JAMES SCHOOLCRAFT SHERMAN II
NOV. 26, 1908 — JULY 29, 1965

American Legion metal flag holders flank the mausoleum entrance in honor of Legionnaire Colonel Thomas Moore Sherman.

A similar flag holder stands beside the grave of William Baker Sherman.

A life-size statue of Vice President Sherman is located at the intersection of Memorial Avenue and Genesee Street, Utica, New York. It was dedicated July 21, 1923. The inscription reads:

JAMES SCHOOLCRAFT SHERMAN
VICE PRESIDENT OF THE UNITED STATES
1908 — 1912*
ERECTED BY
THE CITIZENS OF UTICA

*Served as Vice President from March 4, 1909 to October 30, 1912.

Ruth W. Laird Photograph

James Schoolcraft Sherman Statue.

(28)   THOMAS RILEY MARSHALL
March 4, 1913 — March 3, 1921

(Wilson — Two Terms)

Courtesy of Crown Hill Cemetery. Photograph by Ruth W. Laird

Thomas Riley Marshall Mausoleum. The only mausoleum erected in honor and memory of the ancient accepted Scottish Rite Thirty-third Degree, Northern Masonic Jurisdiction.

Thomas Riley Marshall   Chronology
Twenty-Eighth Vice President
(Woodrow Wilson   Two Terms)

1854, Mar. 14	Born at North Manchester, Indiana
1860	Begins education in public schools of North Manchester.
1873	Is graduated from Wabash College with AB Degree and Phi Beta Kappa citation.
1874	Studies Law in office of Walter Olds.
1875	Admitted to the Bar of Whitley County, Indiana.
1876	Earns Master of Arts Degree at Wabash College; opens Law office in Columbia City, Indiana.
1880	Fails to be elected Prosecuting Attorney.
1881	Becomes a Master Mason in Columbia City Lodge #189, F&AM.
1895, Oct. 2	Marries Lois I. Kimsey. Father of one son.
1898, Sep. 20	Receives the 33d Honorary Degree Ancient Accepted Scottish Rite, Northern Masonic Jurisdiction.
1908	Elected to first of two terms as Governor of Indiana.
1909	LLD Honorary from Wabash College.
1910	LLD Honorary from Notre Dame University.
1911	LLD Honorary from University of Pennsylvania; Coroneted active Sovereign Grand Inspector General, Ancient Accepted Scottish Rite, Northern Masonic Jurisdiction, 33d Degree.
1912	Elected for first term as Vice President.

1913	LLD Honorary from the University of North Carolina.
1914	LLD Honorary from the University of Maine.
1916	Re-elected Vice President of the United States.
1917	LLD Honorary from Washington Jefferson College.
1918	LLD Honorary from Villa Nova College.
1919	Refuses to assume Presidential duties during the serious illness of President Wilson.
1921	Returns to private practice of Law.
1922	Delegate to Supreme Council International Ancient Accepted Scottish Rite, Lausanne, Switzerland.
1924	Prepares manuscript for the publication of *Recollections*.
1925, June 1	Expires in Washington, DC while on a business trip. Age 71 years.
1926	Bronze bust and personal library placed in Marshall Room, Wabash College Library.
1927, Sep. 6	Body placed in mausoleum which was a gift of the Supreme Council, Ancient Accepted Scottish Rite, NMJ, located in the Crown Hill Cemetery, Indianapolis, Indiana.
1928	Bronze plaque on the Garfinkle Store, North Manchester, Indiana reads:

THOMAS RILEY MARSHALL
VICE PRESIDENT
1913–1921
Governor
of
Indiana
BORN ON
THIS SPOT
1854

1979   North Manchester Rotary Club banner carries the message: Birthplace of Thomas R. Marshall, Woodrow Wilson's V.P.

The burial plot of Vice President Thomas Riley Marshall is located in the Crown Hill Cemetery, Indianapolis, Indiana. The memorial monument is centered in an isosceles triangle formed by the avenues separating sections twelve, twenty-three, and forty-six of Crown Hill. The lot, measuring one hundred twenty by one hundred twenty by ninety feet, is the most desirable in the cemetery. It was purchased by the Supreme Council, Ancient Accepted Scottish Rite, 33d Degree, Northern Masonic Jurisdiction located in Boston, Massachusetts. This same body engaged the services of Worshipful Brother Ralph C. Blocksom of Boston to design and build a memorial mausoleum on the site.

Constructed of white Barre granite, it is seventeen and one half feet long and ten feet wide, resting on a foot-high base above the foundation. From floor to roof it measures eight feet six inches. Facing east, the entrance doors are made of bronze six feet six inches high and nineteen inches wide. Flanking the entrance are two urns and a hedge of yew shrubbery. Above the door, in five-inch high letters, is the name

THOMAS R. MARSHALL

There are two leaded stained glass windows in the rear, each eighteen inches wide and three feet high.

The vault of the mausoleum contains three crypts on either side. On the right, looking in, the crypt on the bottom is inscribed:

MORRISON MARSHALL
1916 — 1920

The middle crypt is inscribed:

THOMAS RILEY MARSHALL
MARCH 14, 1854–JUNE 1, 1925

The top:

LOIS IRENE MARSHALL
MAY 8, 1873–JANUARY 6, 1958

On the left side, looking in, the top crypt has this inscription:

MARTHA A. MARSHALL
1829–1854

The middle:

DANIEL M. MARSHALL, MD
1823–1892

There is no inscription on the bottom crypt.

It is interesting to note that Vice President Marshall's funeral service was conducted by Masons, and that this impressive monument was a gift of the Supreme Council of the Ancient Accepted Scottish Rite; but nowhere can be found one symbol of this highly symbolic fraternity, nor indication that a Vice President was buried here.

The burial service at Crown Hill Cemetery was conducted by the Ancient Landmarks Lodge, AF&AM, and the Illustrious Brother's body placed in the mausoleum September 6, 1927.

(29)   CALVIN COOLIDGE
March 4, 1921 — August 2, 1923

(Harding)

Succeeded to the Presidency upon death of Harding

Courtesy of Plymouth Notch Village Cemetery. Photograph by Ruth W. Laird

Coolidge Grave Monuments

Calvin Coolidge   Chronology
Twenty-Ninth Vice President
(Warren G. Harding)

1872, July 4	Born at Plymouth Notch, Vermont.
1877	Attends old stone schoolhouse just north of birthplace.
1886	Enrolls in Black River Academy, Ludlow, Vermont.
1890	Is graduated from Black River Academy.
1895	Is graduated from Amherst College, Cum Laude; delivers Grove Oration; receives Sons of American Revolution Gold Medal. Begins to study Law.
1897	Admitted to the Bar.
1898	Opens Law office and becomes Northampton Councilman.
1899	City Solicitor.
1904	Clerk of Courts.
1905, Oct. 4	Marries Grace Anna Goodhue. Father of two sons.
1907	State Legislator.
1910	Mayor of Northhampton.
1912	Massachusetts Senator.
1914	President of Massachusetts Senate.
1916	Lieutenant Governor of Massachusetts.
1919	Governor of Massachusetts; gains national prominence by dramatic settling of Boston police strike.
1920	Elected Vice President of the United States.

1923, Aug. 2	Succeeds to the office of President upon death of Warren G. Harding; takes oath of Office in his father's home, Plymouth, Vermont. Father administers oath at 2:47 a.m. Aug. 3.
1924, July 7	Youngest son expires in White House.
1924, Nov.	Elected President of the United States.
1927	Announces that he does not choose to run for another term as President.
1929	Approves Kellogg-Briand Pact; begins to write autobiography.
1930	Purchases "The Beeches"; publishes articles on current events.
1933, Jan. 5	Passes away in his home in Northampton, Massachusetts, age 60.
1956	Homestead property at Plymouth Notch, Vermont given to the State of Vermont by surviving son, John Coolidge.
1971	Visitor's Center opened near birthplace.
1978	Ludlow Rotary Club immortalizes the Black River Academy, Calvin Coolidge, the 29th Vice President and 30th President, and Paul Harris, founder of Rotary International, by placing likenesses on the club banner. Both Coolidge and Harris attended the Black River Academy.

An unpretentious headstone dominated by the Seal of the President of the United States marks the grave of Calvin Coolidge, the twenty-ninth Vice President of the United States.

Photograph by Ruth W. Laird

CALVIN COOLIDGE
1872-1933
Born July 4, 1872 in a house back of store, Calvin Coolidge from 4 years of age lived in the Homestead across the road, now owned by the State of Vermont. Here on Aug. 3, 1923 he was inaugurated President and here he spent many vacations. In the Notch Cemetery he rests beside his wife & son and 4 generations of forebears.

Coolidge Historical Marker erected by the State of Vermont.

The monument is located in the Village Cemetery at Plymouth Notch, Vermont and is inscribed:

CALVIN COOLIDGE
JULY 4, 1872
JANUARY 5, 1933

As one faces President Coolidge's headstone, to the right is a smaller headstone, the same in design, with a wreath replacing the Presidential Seal. The headstone carries this inscription:

CALVIN
COOLIDGE
JUNIOR
***
APRIL 13, 1908
JULY 7, 1924

As one faces the grave of President Coolidge, the headstone of Mrs. Coolidge is located on the left. This headstone is of the same size and design as that of the President. A wreath replaces the Presidential Seal. The tombstone bears the following inscription:

GRACE A. GOODHUE
WIFE OF
CALVIN COOLIDGE
JANUARY 3, 1879
JULY 8, 1957

A State of Vermont Historical Marker records the following:

CALVIN COOLIDGE
1872   1933
Born July 4, 1872 in a house back
of store, Calvin Coolidge from 4
years of age lived in the Homestead
across the road, now owned by the
State of Vermont. Here on Aug. 3,
1923 he was inaugurated President
and here he spent many vacations.
In the Notch Cemetery he rests
beside his wife & son and 4
generations of forebears.

(30)   CHARLES GATES DAWES
March 4, 1925 — March 3, 1929

(Coolidge — Second Term)

Courtesy of Rose Hill Cemetery.

Charles Gates Dawes Mausoleum.

Charles Gates Dawes   Chronology   Thirtieth Vice President
(Coolidge   Second Term)

1865, Aug. 27	Born at Marietta, Ohio.
1884	Receives Bachelor of Arts Degree from Marietta College.
1886	Cincinnati Law School student.
1887	Receives Master of Arts Degree from Marietta College.
	Opens Law office in Lincoln, Nebraska.
1889, Jan. 24	Marries Caro D. Blymer. Father of two children.
1893	Financial panic plunges him deeply into debt.
1894	Public Utilities executive; author of "Banking System in the United States".
1895	Moves to Chicago and enters public utility field.
1896	Republican Executive Committee member.
1897	Comptroller of the U.S. Treasury.
1902	Defeated in contest for U.S. Senate; organizes Central Trust Company of Illinois and becomes its president.
1910	Composes "Melody in A Major".
1917	Major, U.S. Army; Chairman, General Purchasing Board of the American Expeditionary Forces, France.
1918, Oct.	Brigadier General.
1919	Awarded Distinguished Service Medal; receives military citations from Great Britain, Belgium, France, and Italy. Resigns from the U.S. Army.

1921	First Director, U.S. Bureau of the Mint.
1923	Formulates Dawes Plan for German Reparations.
1924	Elected Vice President of the United States.
1925	Joint winner of Nobel Peace Prize with Sir Austin Chamberlain.
1929	Ambassador to Great Britain.
1932, Jan.	President, Reconstruction Finance Corporation.
1932, June	Resigns from Reconstruction Finance Corporation and obtains loan for his financially troubled City National Bank and Trust Company.
1933	Promotes Chicago World's Fair.
1935	Author *Notes as Vice President*.
1939	Author *Journal of Reparations, Journal as Ambassador to Great Britain*.
1939	Memorial dedicated in Hall of History, Forest Lawn Cemetery, Glendale California.

The tribute, recorded on a stone tablet, states:

CHARLES GATES DAWES
SOLDIER   STATESMAN
HUMANITARIAN
"A man who has placed his name high
among the great of the world in this
generation because he ruled his life by
common sense."
"That Man Dawes" by Paul R. Leach

1951, Apr. 23	Expires at his home in Evanston, Illinois at the age of 85.
1952	Dawes home, built in 1894, a French Gothic mansion of 28 rooms, with a theater, ballroom, and formal gardens, becomes the headquarters of the Evanston Historical Society.

Courtesy of Evanston Historical Society

Charles G. Dawes Residence.

1977   Home becomes an Historic Landmark. The
                       tablet reads:

The residence of Charles Gates Dawes
1865–1951
Soldier, Statesman, Diplomat, Banker
Vice President of the United States
Given by him to the
Northwestern University
With the hope that it might become the
Home of the Evanston Historical Society
This memorial placed here
By the tablet section of
The Evanston Historical Society
1963
Evanston Centennial Year

The monument marking the grave of Charles Gates Dawes is
located in section one hundred two, just east of the Rosehill
Cemetery chapel in Chicago. The lot on which it stands contains over three thousand square feet, having a forty-five-foot
front and a depth of eighty feet.

The building is a small Greek temple mausoleum approximately fourteen feet wide and twenty-one feet long. The front
entablature is supported by four Doric order columns, each
nine feet high, facing north.

The entrance is guarded by two bronze doors, each seven feet
high and twenty-one inches wide. The approach is by two steps
seven inches high to the first landing, ten feet wide and six feet
long. Four more steps lead to the entrance platform. All steps
are flanked by twenty-two-inch wide blocks of granite.

Above the bronze doors, in six-inch high letters, is the word

DAWES

In the rear of the mausoleum is a stained glass window four feet high and two and one half feet wide.

The vault of the mausoleum contains four crypts. The lower crypt on the west side is inscribed:

Rufus Dawes
Died September 5, 1912
Age 21 years, 8 months 21 days.

The upper crypt, east side:

CHARLES G. DAWES
Died April 23, 1951
Age 85 years 7 months 27 days.

The lower crypt, east side:

Caro D. B. Dawes
Died October 3, 1957
Age 92 Years.

(31)   CHARLES CURTIS
March 4, 1929 — March 3, 1933

(Hoover)

Courtesy of Topeka Cemetery. Maria C. Sanchez Photograph

CHARLES CURTIS
VICE-PRESIDENT, UNITED STATES
1929 ———— 1933

Charles Curtis Monument.

Charles Curtis   Chronology
Thirty-First Vice President
(Hoover)

1860, Jan. 25	Born in North Topeka, Kansas.
1863–66	Lives with grandmother, Permelia Hubbard Curtis.
1866–69	Lives on Kaw Indian Reservation, educated in mission school.
1870	Rides as jockey at Kansas fairs.
1874	On way to an Indian Reservation in Indian Territory. Grandmother Pappan persuades him not to be a "Blanket Indian".
1875	Finishes common school and signs contract as jockey at $50 per month, with a percentage of winnings.
1876	Ends "jockey" contract. Enters high school; conducts livery business.
1879	Is graduated from high school; class orator. Begins study of Law in the office of A. H. Case, Esquire.
1881	Admitted to the Bar.
1884, Nov. 27	Marries Annie E. Baird. Father of three children.
1885	Shawnee County Attorney.
1889	Fails to win seat in Congress.
1892	Elected to Congress, first of three terms.
1907, Jan. 29	Sworn in as U.S. Senator. President Pro-Tempore December 4-12, 1911.
1913, May 13	Term in Senate expires.
1914	Elected to the U.S. Senate under the 17th Amendment, ratified May 13, 1913.

1917	Advocates Women's Rights. Opposes Preparedness.
1918	Supports Woman Suffrage.
1919	Opposes the League of Nations.
1920	Re-elected to the Senate.
1924, June 21	Wife passes away.
1929, Mar. 4	Vice President of the United States.
1933	Opens Law office in Washington, D.C.
1936, Feb. 8	Expires in the Nation's capital at the age of 76 years.
1978	Kansas Historical Highway Marker on route 24 near the site of the Kansa Indian Agency states that the U.S. Government erected a stone house for White Plume, head chief of the Kansa, who was great, great grandfather of Vice President Charles Curtis.

The grave of Charles Curtis is located in section eighty on number two road of the Topeka, Kansas Cemetery. It is easily located by entering the cemetery from California Avenue and going north to the A. A. Hurd mausoleum. At this circle is a fifteen-foot high flag pole on the road side of the twelve-foot wide and fifteen-foot deep Curtis burial plot.

The monument is of granite four feet seven inches long, three feet high, and sixteen inches wide. Facing west the monument has two-inch high letters:

CHARLES CURTIS
VICE-PRESIDENT, UNITED STATES
1929 — 1933

The rear is inscribed in five-inch high letters

CURTIS

Seven feet to the east of the plot monument are flat head stones two feet by one foot, with the one on the south reading:

CHARLES
CURTIS
1860–1936

and the one on the north:

ANNIE BAIRD
CURTIS
1860–1924

(32)   JOHN NANCE GARNER
March 4, 1933 — January 20, 1941

(Franklin Delano Roosevelt — First & Second Terms)

Photo by Ed Habey.

John N. Garner Monument.

John Nance Garner   Chronology
Thirty-Second Vice President
(Franklin D. Roosevelt   First and Second Terms)

1868, Nov. 22	Born at Blossom Prairie, Red River County, Texas
1874–77	Attends elementary school to the fourth grade.
1878	Store clerk; farm hand.
1887	Attends Vanderbilt University.
1888	Studies Law, Clarksville, Texas.
1890	Admitted to the Bar; opens Law office, Clarksville.
1891	Moves to Uvalde, Texas.
1892	Edits weekly newspaper.
1893	Rancher; acquires ownership of two banks. County Judge
1895, Nov. 25	Marries Marietta Rheiner. Father of one child.
1898	Elected to Texas Legislature.
1902	Elected U.S. Congressman for first of fifteen consecutive terms.
1921	Chairman, House Ways and Means Committee.
1928	House Floor Leader.
1931	Chairman, House Ways and Means Committee.
1932	Speaker of the House of Representatives.
1933	Vice President of the United States. For the second time in U.S. history the House Speaker becomes Vice President.
1936	Elected Vice President for second term. Receives LLB Honorary Degree from John Marshall College and Baylor University.

1940	Opposes third term decision of Franklin D. Roosevelt. Fails to receive Democratic nomination for President.
1941, Jan. 20	Retires from politics.
1948, Aug. 17	Wife passes away.
1967, Nov. 7	Expires at his home in Uvalde at the age of 98 years, eleven months, fifteen days.

The grave of John Nance Garner, thirty-second Vice President of the United States, is located in the Uvalde Cemetery, Uvalde, Texas. His grave monument has a center polished granite stone forty-two inches high and thirty inches wide. Its upper half contains a replica of the Seal of the Vice President of the United States. Beneath the seal is a quotation from one of his speeches:

> "THERE ARE JUST TWO THINGS TO THIS
> GOVERNMENT AS I SEE IT — THE FIRST IS TO
> SAFEGUARD THE LIVES AND PROPERTIES
> OF OUR PEOPLE — THE SECOND IS TO INSURE
> THAT EACH OF US HAS A CHANCE TO WORK OUT
> HIS DESTINY ACCORDING TO HIS TALENTS."
> JNO. N. GARNER

The right flanking stone, as one looks at the monument, is inscribed:

> MARIETTA RHEINER
> GARNER
> JULY 17, 1869
> AUG. 17, 1948

The left flanking stone is inscribed:

> JOHN NANCE
> GARNER
> NOV 22, 1868
> NOV 7, 1967

In front of the grave monument is a bronze plaque erected by the Texas State Historical Committee which reads:

JOHN NANCE GARNER
(NOVEMBER 22, 1868–NOVEMBER 7, 1967)
VICE PRESIDENT OF THE U.S. 1933–1941
BEGAN CAREER AS UVALDE COUNTY
JUDGE 1893–1896. SERVED IN TEXAS
LEGISLATURE 1898–1902; IN U.S.
CONGRESS 1904–1932, WHERE HE WAS,
IN LAST TERM, SPEAKER OF HOUSE
OF REPRESENTATIVES. ALSO AN ABLE
TRIAL LAWYER, RANCHER, BANKER AND
BENEFACTOR OF SOUTHWEST TEXAS
JUNIOR COLLEGE. MARRIED ETTIE
RHEINER. HAD A SON, TULLY: ONE
GRANDCHILD, GENEVIEVE C. CURRIE.
KNOWN AS "CACTUS JACK" FOR HIS
UNIQUE WESTERN INDIVIDUALISM.
RECORDED 1968

(33)   HENRY AGARD WALLACE
January 20, 1941 — January 20, 1945

(Franklin Delano Roosevelt — Third Term)

Photo by Helen M. Phillips.

Henry A. Wallace Monument.

Henry Agard Wallace   Chronology
Thirty-Third Vice President
(Franklin Delano Roosevelt   Third Term)

1888, Oct. 7	Born in Adair County, Iowa.
1895	Moves with parents to Des Moines, Iowa.
1904	Challenges the "blue ribbon corn" theory and begins a thirty-year campaign against "pretty ear corn" shows.
1906	Is graduated from the Old West High School.
1908	Develops hybrid corn seed.
1910	Earns Bachelor of Science degree at Iowa State College; associate editor *Wallaces' Farmer*.
1913	Cross fertilizes Boone County white and Wisconsin corn.
1914, May 20	Marries Ilo Browne. Father of three children.
1920	Master of Science, Honorary, Iowa State College.
1924	Editor *Wallaces' Farmer*; Copper Cross hybrid corn wins gold medal.
1926	Founds Pioneer Hi-Bred Corn Company.
1927, Oct. 4	Becomes a Master Mason in Capital Lodge #110, AF&AM, Des Moines.
1929	Editor *Wallaces' Farmer* and *Iowa Homestead*.
1933	Secretary of Agriculture.
1934	Receives Doctor of Science, Honorary, Iowa State College.
1941	Vice President of the United States.
1942	"Common Man" speech hailed as greatest oration since the Gettysburg Address.
1943	Author of "The Century of the Common Man."

1945   Secretary of Commerce.

1946, Jan.   Outlines Economic Bill of Rights before
                 Senate Committee.

1946, Sep. 12   Delivery of prior approved speech results
                 in summary dismissal as Secretary of Com-
                 merce.

1947   Editor of *New Republic.* Book entitled *"Hy-
                 brid Corn Makers"* states that "Wallace
                 provided the outstanding genetic achieve-
                 ment of our time." Tours western Europe.

1948   Progressive Party candidate for President. Not
                 elected.

1949   Begins genetic experiments with poultry,
                 strawberries, and gladioli.

1965, Nov. 18   Expires in Danbury, Connecticut at the age of
                 77 years.

Photograph by Ruth W. Laird

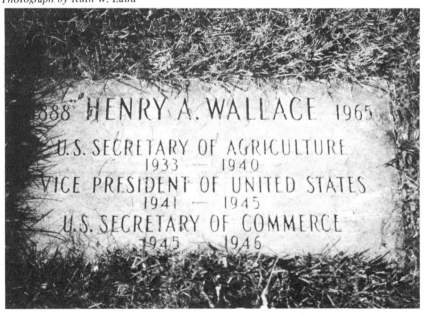

Henry A. Wallace headstone

1970	Commemorative poem published by Durk D. Offringa.*
1978	State of Iowa Agriculture Building in Des Moines named the Henry A. Wallace Building.

*A TRIBUTE TO HENRY A. WALLACE:

"A giant leap for all mankind
Was made by Wallace when
He crossed the genes of inbred stock
For hybrid corn and hen.
Such genes were known for centuries,
But Wallace took the lead
To make the hybrid principle
a hungry world to feed.

"No man in history has done more
Than Henry Wallace did
For people anywhere on earth
More needed food to get,
For those who like a low-cost treat
For families big or small,
Fresh eggs and chicken dinners are
Available for all.

"So let us pause to honor him
As scientist, as friend
Of common people everywhere,
In every continent
As great humanitarian,
World citizen who ranks
Amongst the greatest of the age,
To H. A. Wallace — Thanks!"
            June 1970 Hy-Line International Letter.

The monument marking the grave of Henry Agard Wallace is located in section thirty-one of the Glendale Cemetery, University Avenue at Forty Eighth Street, Des Moines, Iowa.

The burial plot is twenty-four feet wide and forty-two feet deep. The granite monument is located at the rear of the plot with these measurements: The crown is six feet long, thirty inches high, and ten inches wide, resting on a granite base eight feet long, nineteen inches wide, and one foot high. It faces east and is flanked by Japanese yew shrubbery.

The inscription front and rear, in four-inch high letters, reads:

WALLACE

Eight feet east of the plot monument is a two-foot by one-foot stone flush with the turf which is inscribed:

1888 HENRY A. WALLACE 1965
U.S. SECRETARY OF AGRICULTURE
1933–1940
VICE PRESIDENT OF UNITED STATES
1941–1945
U.S. SECRETARY OF COMMERCE
1945–1946

Thirty feet east of the plot monument is a stone flush with the turf reading:

VIRGINIA S. WALLACE
1895–1951

(34)   HARRY S. TRUMAN
January 20, 1945 — April 12, 1945

(Franklin Delano Roosevelt — Fourth Term)

Succeeded to the Presidency upon death of F. D. Roosevelt

Courtesy of Harry S. Truman Library. Ruth W. Laird Photograph.

Truman Memorial Ledger.

Harry S. Truman   Chronology
Thirty-Fourth Vice President
(Franklin D. Roosevelt   Fourth Term)

1884, May 8	Born at Lamar, Missouri.
1890	Student in public school.
1894	Drug store clerk.
1900	Denied admission to West Point because of defective vision.
1901	Newspaper reporter, railroad timekeeper, bank clerk.
1905	Enlists in the Missouri National Guard.
1906	Farmer.
1909, Mar. 18	Becomes a Master Mason in Belmont Lodge #450, F&AM, Grandview, MO.
1917	Called to active military duty with Field Artillery Unit of the Missouri National Guard, commissioned Lieutenant.
1918	Captain, American Expeditionary Forces, France.
1919, June 28	Marries Elizabeth Virginia Wallace. Father of one child.
1920	Major, Missouri National Guard.
1922	Haberdashery store bankrupt.
1923	Judge, Jackson County Court (an administrator); studies Law.
1924, Feb. 17	Daughter born.
1926	Presiding Judge, Jackson County until 1934.
1932	Colonel, United States Army Reserve.
1934	Elected United States Senator, first of two terms.
1939	Honorary Past Grand Master, Order of DeMolay.

1940	Right Worshipful Grand Master of the Grand Lodge, AF & AM, of Missouri.
1941	Heads Truman Commission to investigate defense expenditures.
1944	Elected Vice President of the United States.
1945, Apr. 12	Succeeds to the Presidency. Launches the United Nations.
1945, Oct. 19	Coroneted Sovereign Grand Inspector General, Ancient Accepted Scottish Rite, Southern Masonic Jurisdiction, 33d Degree.
1945	Recipient of the Gourgas Medal. The first individual to be so honored by the Supreme Council of the Ancient Accepted Scottish Rite, 33d Degree Northern Masonic Jurisdiction.
1946, Sep. 12	Dismisses Secretary of Commerce Henry A. Wallace who had delivered a previously approved speech. Issues Truman Doctrine to oppose Communism.
1947	Vetoes Taft-Hartley Law.
1948, April	Orders the Berlin Airlift.
	Elected President of the United States
1949, Jan. 20	Sworn in as President with Alben W. Barkley as Vice President.
1950, Jan.	Approves H-Bomb Project.
	Master of Missouri Lodge of Research, F & AM.
1950, June	Commits United States Troops in Korean Conflict.
1950, Nov. 1	Target of futile assassination attempt.
1951, April 11	Exercises Constitutional power to relieve the Supreme Commander of Allied Forces in Korea. General MacArthur, who was relieved, states that the action was "done in a way which amounted to drastic summary punishment. . . . This was no mere change of command — It was vengeful reprisal."

1952, Mar. 30	Japanese Peace Treaty becomes effective.
1953, Jan. 20	Retires to his home in Independence, Missouri.
1955	Author of Volume I, *Years of Decisions.*
1956	Author of Volume II, *Years of Decision — Years of Trial and Hope.* Receives Honorary Degree from Oxford University. Only child marries.
1957	Dedicates the Harry S. Truman Library, Independence, Missouri.
1964	Picture of birthplace appears on the silk banner of the Lamar, Missouri Rotary Club.
1972, Dec. 26	Expires in hospital in Kansas City, Missouri at the age of 88 years.
1973	Picture of the Harry S. Truman Library graces the silk banner of the Independence Rotary Club.
1976, May 8	Life-sized walking statue by Gilbert Franklin dedicated just outside the window of his office in the Jackson County Court House where he was Presiding Judge of Jackson County, Missouri. On the four-foot high, three-foot wide pedestal is this inscription:

HARRY S. TRUMAN
1884 — 1972
PRESIDENT
of the
UNITED STATES
1945 — 1953

The burial plot of Harry S. Truman, the thirty-fourth Vice President of the United States, is located in the courtyard of the Harry S. Truman Library and Museum, Independence, Missouri.

The space allotted for graves, twelve feet square, is surrounded by a pavement creating a square enclosure approximately thirty-three feet on each side. President Truman is buried in the north side of the plot, with the top of the Memorial Ledger toward the west and the bottom toward the east.

The inscription on the horizontal stone slab monument is as follows:

HARRY S. TRUMAN
BORN MAY 8, 1884
LAMAR, MISSOURI
DIED DECEMBER 26, 1972

MARRIED JUNE 28, 1919
DAUGHTER
BORN FEBRUARY 17, 1924

JUDGE
EASTERN DISTRICT
JACKSON COUNTY
JAN. 1, 1923 — JAN. 1, 1925
PRESIDING JUDGE
JACKSON COUNTY
JAN. 1, 1927 — JAN. 1, 1935
UNITED STATES SENATOR
MISSOURI
JAN. 3, 1935 — JAN. 18, 1945
VICE-PRESIDENT
UNITED STATES
JAN. 20, 1945 — APRIL 12, 1945
PRESIDENT
UNITED STATES
APRIL 12, 1945 — JAN. 20, 1953

Photograph by Ruth W. Laird

Truman Walking Statue. Courthouse Square, Independence, Mo.

The Seal of the President of the United States is above the name, Harry S. Truman, and the Seal of the United States Senate and the Seal of Jackson County, Missouri are at the bottom of the ledger on the right and left sides, respectively.

The memorial ledger is a white granite slab, eight feet long, three feet six inches wide, eight inches thick, weighing thirty-seven hundred pounds. The Presidential Seal has a three dimensional appearance. The edges of the slab are beveled.

The material of the Harry S. Truman ledger is select Barre granite, quarried at Barre, Vermont. All of the carving and lettering was hand done, and required eight weeks to complete.

(35)   ALBEN WILLIAM BARKLEY
January 20, 1949 — January 20, 1953

(Truman — Second Term)

Courtesy of Mount Kenton Cemetery. Ruth W. Laird Photograph

Alben William Barkley Monument.

Alben William Barkley Chronology
Thirty-Fifth Vice President
(Truman Second Term)

1877, Nov. 24	Born at Lowes, Graves County, Kentucky.
1893	Wins many declamation contests and debates in high school.
1897	Earns Bachelor of Arts Degree at Marvin College, Clinton, Kentucky.
	Is college janitor as an undergraduate.
1898	Attends Emory College, Oxford, Georgia.
1899	Law student, University of Virginia, Charlottesville, Virginia.
1901	Admitted to the Bar. Opens Law office in Paducah, Kentucky.
1902	Joins Beneficial, Protective Order of Elks Lodge #217.
1903, June 23	Marries Dorothy Brower. Father of three children.
1905	Prosecuting Attorney.
1909	McCracken County Judge.
1913	Begins first of four terms in the United States Congress.
1927	United States Senator. Serves until January 1949.
1947, Mar. 10	First wife passes away.
1949	Becomes Vice President of the United States. Marries Jane Hadley November 18th.
1954	Elected U.S. Senator.
1956, Apr. 30	Expires in Lexington, Virginia at the age of 78 years.

1957	Alben W. Barkley Room dedicated in the Margaret I. King Library, University of Kentucky, Lexington.
1962, March	By this time Kentucky Historical Highway Markers numbered 680, 829, 840, 891, 916, 918, 1025, 1029, 1030, 1112, 1214 have been erected in his memory.
1963, Oct. 3	Life-sized bronze statue, executed by Walter Hancock, supported on a marble base, unveiled in the rotunda of the State Capitol. The rotunda is modeled after that of the Hotel des Invalides in Paris with the arched ceiling and the circular balustrade above the crypt of Napoleon. The Frankfort Capitol rotunda contains the statues of five great Kentuckians. In the center is Lincoln. At the entrance, in the southeast, is Henry Clay. In clockwise direction, Jefferson Davis, Ephraim McDowell, M.D., and Alben William Barkley, northwest:

Born November 24, 1877
Died April 30, 1956
Member of the United States House
and Senate. Majority leader of the
United States Senate, Vice President
of the United States.

1965, Nov. 24	Everett McKinley Dirksen pays tribute when Barkley's statue is unveiled in the King Library, University of Kentucky at Lexington.
1966	Kentucky Historical Highway Marker #573 at Barkley's Birthplace, near Mayfield, Graves County reads:
	"Alben W. Barkley, U.S. Senator and Vice President, was born near here, November 24, 1877. A life long leader in the

Democratic Party. Elected Prosecuting Attorney for McCracken Co., in 1905. County Judge 1909, Congressman 1913, and U.S. Senator 1927. Majority leader of Senate longer than any other man. Vice President 1949–53. Elected Senator 1954. Death April 30, 1956.''

In the Maplewood cemetery in Mayfield are the world famous monuments, a strange procession that never moves. There are sixteen statues surrounding the grave of Henry Wooldridge, known as the Wooldridge Monuments.

1972, Oct. 19   Barkley home in Paducah established as an historical public attraction.

The grave of Alben William Barkley is located in the Mt. Kenton Cemetery on Lone Oak Road, Paducah, Kentucky. The grave monument has a concrete base eleven feet long, four feet wide, and one foot high. This foundation supports the monument base, nine feet six inches long, and the crown, eight feet long, three feet four inches high, and fourteen inches wide.

The front and rear inscription, in five-inch high letters:

BARKLEY

Facing the monument, the flat head stone on the left reads:

ALBEN WILLIAM
BARKLEY
NOVEMBER 24, 1877
APRIL 30, 1956

The one on the right:

DOROTHY BROWER
BARKLEY
NOVEMBER 14, 1882
MARCH 10, 1947

To the far right:

DAVID BARKLEY
HOLLOWAY
AUGUST 9, 1970

The corners of the forty by thirty-six foot burial plot are marked by yew bushes.

A Kentucky Highway Historical Marker at the entrance to the Mt. Kenton Cemetery, Paducah, McCracken County reads:

Alben W. Barkley, Vice President of the United States, 1949–53. Member U.S. Senate, 1927–49 and 1955–56; Senate Democratic leader 13 years; House of Representatives 1913–27. Born Lowes, Ky., 1877. Came to Paducah 1898. Elected to first public office as McCracken County attorney, 1905. County Judge, 1909. Buried in Mt. Kenton Cemetery, in 1956. Loved and honored by nation.

Alben W. Barkley, "The Veep" was senate majority leader under Pres. Franklin D. Roosevelt, and Vice-Pres. under President Harry S. Truman. He died April 30, 1956 while addressing a mock Democratic Convention at Washington and Lee Univ. His last words were: "I would rather be a servant in the house of the Lord than sit in the seats of the mighty."

Kentucky Historical Markers honor Vice President Barkley in various places in the state. At the corner of 28th and Jefferson Streets, Paducah, a grey marble block seven feet high and four feet square carries the silhouette of Barkley and this inscription on all four sides:

"I would rather be a servant in the house of the Lord than sit in the seats of the mighty."

ALBEN W. BARKLEY
1877 –1956

This memorial was sponsored by the Paducah Junior Chamber of Commerce and the Kentucky State Federation of Labor.

Photograph by Ruth W. Laird

Barkley Silhouette Obelisk.

Photograph by Ruth W. Laird

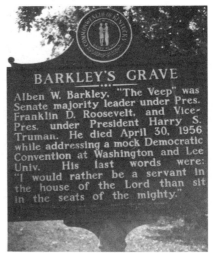

Kentucky Historical Highway Marker.

Courtesy of Mount Kenton Cemetery

Alben W. Barkley Headstone.

Ruth W. Laird Photographs

Headstone of Barkley Grandson.

Kentucky Historical Society Photo.

Barkley Statue in Kentucky State Capitol Rotunda, Frankfort, KY

(36)   RICHARD MILHOUS NIXON
January 20, 1953 — January 20, 1961

(Eisenhower — Two Terms)

Richard Milhous Nixon   Chronology
Thirty-Sixth Vice President
(Eisenhower   Two Terms)

1913, Jan. 9	Born at Yorba Linda, California.
1926–28	Student at Fullerton High School.
1928–30	Student at Whittier High School. Wins oratorical contest in senior year.
1934	Is graduated from Whittier College; earns Bachelor of Arts Degree and scholarship to Duke University Law School.
1936	Elected to the Order of Coif (The Law equivalent to Alpha Omega Alpha in Medicine and Phi Beta Kappa in undergraduate school.)
1937	Earns LLB Degree at Duke. Admitted to the Bar in California and opens Law Office in Whittier.
1938	Establishes frozen orange juice business.
1939	Orange juice business fails.
1940, June 21	Marries Thelma Catherine Patricia Ryan. Father of two daughters.
1942	Attorney for Office of Emergency Management; begins military service in World War II as Lieutenant Junior Grade, United States Navy.
1943	Promoted to Lieutenant, U.S. Navy.
1945	Discharged from Navy as Lieutenant Commander, USNR.
1946	Elected to Congress.
1947	Votes to override the Taft-Hartley Bill veto as first term Congressman.

1948	Re-elected to Congress. Named to House Un-American Activities Committee.
1949	Investigates famous espionage case and wins conviction.
1950	Elected to the Senate.
1951	Condemns summary dismissal of General MacArthur.
1952	Elected Vice President of the United States.
1953	Honorary member of Whittier Rotary Club. Tours the Far East.
1953	Promoted to Commander, United States Naval Reserve.
1954	Delivers commencement address at Whittier College.
1955, Sept.	Almost an acting President due to serious illness of President Eisenhower.
1956, June 8	Almost an acting President due to serious illness of President Eisenhower.
1956, Nov.	Re-elected Vice President.
1957, Nov. 25	Almost an acting President due to the serious illness of President Eisenhower.
1958	Mobs endanger life in Venezuela.
1959	Visits Russia. Family home in Yorba Linda dedicated by the town as an Historic Site.
1960	Defeated in race for the office of President.
1961	Defeated in race for the office of California Governor.
1962	Author of best selling book *Six Crises*.
1963	Begins the practice of Law in New York City.
1964	Declines overtures to run for the office of Vice President.
1967, Mar.	Travels to Europe and the Soviet Union. Has an audience with Pope Paul VI.
1967, Aug.	Travels in the Far East.
1968	Elected President of the United States.

1969, Oct. 10	Announces intention of naming Lieutenant General Lewis B. Hershey advisor to the President on Manpower Mobilization. Before the year's end four men land on the moon. Orders destructive bombing in North Viet Nam.
1970, Feb. 16	Lewis B. Hershey becomes a four-star General upon Presidential recommendation. Air Force ROTC enrolls women.
1971	Kentucky Historical Highway Marker #1419, near Simpsonville states that "President Nixon delivered grave side eulogy for Whitney M. Young, Jr. First civil rights leader to be so honored." Committee for the Re-election of the President formed.
1972	Dedicates American Museum of Immigration at the base of the Statue of Liberty, Liberty Island, New York. Visits Communist China. Re-elected President.
1973	Viet Nam War winds down. Military draft ends. Watergate Cover-up and White House tape controversy begin. Army ROTC enrolls women.
1973, Oct. 10	Vice President Agnew resigns.
1973, Oct. 12	Appoints Congressman Gerald R. Ford to fill the vacancy in the office of Vice President.
1973, Oct. 20	"Saturday Night Massacre" occurs.
1974, Jan.	Tells the Nation that "One year of Watergate is enough," and that he will not resign.
1974, Aug. 9	Resigns as President of the United States.
1974, Sep. 8	Receives "Blanket Pardon" from President Ford.
1974	Returns to home in Southern California.
1978, Jan.	Attends Hubert H. Humphrey memorial service in Washington, D.C. Publishes *Memoirs*.

1978, Nov.   Visits France, and delivers lecture at Oxford University, London, England.

1979, Jan. 29   Visits the White House through an invitation from President Carter to meet the Vice Premier of China.

(37)   LYNDON BAINES JOHNSON
January 20, 1961 — November 22, 1963

(Kennedy)

Succeeded to the Presidency upon death of Kennedy.

Courtesy of Lyndon Baines Johnson Historic Site. Ruth W. Laird Photograph

Lyndon Baines Johnson Grave Monument.

Lyndon Baines Johnson   Chronology
Thirty-Seventh Vice President
(John F. Kennedy)

1908, Aug. 27	Born near Stonewall, Texas.
1914	Begins education in the public grade school of Albert, Texas. It was here that he said: "Someday I'm going to be President of the United States."
1924	Is graduated from the Fredericksburg High School.
1930	Earns B.S. Degree at Southwest Texas State Teachers College.
1931	Teacher of Speech in the public schools of Houston, Texas.
1932	Secretary for Congressman Kleberg, attends Georgetown Law School.
1934, Nov. 17	Marries Claudia Alta Taylor. Father of two daughters.
1935	State Director of National Youth Administration.
1937	U.S. Congressman until "Pearl Harbor".
1941	U.S. Navy duty in the Southwest Pacific Theatre.
1942	Decorated by General Douglas MacArthur.
1943	Returns to Congressional Seat by order of the President.
1949	Begins first of two terms in the U.S. Senate.
1951	Purchases the LBJ Ranch.
1960	Elected Vice President of the United States.
1961, Aug.	Visits Berlin at the request of President Kennedy.

1963, Nov. 22	Succeeds to the Presidency following the assasination of Kennedy; sworn in by Judge Sarah T. Hughes.
1964, Mar.	Visits General Douglas MacArthur who advises that the United States refrain from involvement in a Land War in Asia Minor.
1965	Receives Honorary LLB Degree from the University of Michigan. Launches Land War in Viet Nam.
1967, Feb. 23	25th Amendment to the Constitution ratified.
1967	Signs Act providing medical care for the elderly.
1968	Announces that he will not seek re-election as President.
1969	Author of *Vantage Point*.
1969	Dedicates the Lyndon Baines Johnson National Historic Site near Johnson City, Texas; establishes the LBJ Library on the University of Texas Campus at Austin — the first Presidential Library to be situated on a University Campus.
1973, Jan. 22	Expires at Fort Sam Houston, Texas at the age of 64 years.
1973, Sep.	Fredericksburg, Texas Rotary Club immortalizes Lyndon B. Johnson and Fleet Admiral Chester W. Nimitz by placing their pictures on the Rotary Club banner.
1978, Aug.	A bronze plaque is dedicated in the lobby of the Parkland Memorial Hospital, Dallas, Texas under the portrait of Lyndon Baines Johnson. The inscription reads:

LYNDON BAINES JOHNSON

August 27, 1908 — January 22, 1973

"Dedicated to the memory of a native Texas son, who became the 36th President in the Parkland Memorial Hospital at the death of John F. Kennedy. From this hospital, Lyndon Baines Johnson proceeded to Dallas' Love Field where he took the oath of office as President of the United States aboard Air Force One."

The plaque was a gift of the Hospital Women's Auxiliary.

The monument marking the grave of Lyndon Baines Johnson, the thirty-seventh Vice President of the United States, is located in the Johnson Family Cemetery on the grounds of the LBJ Ranch near Johnson City, Texas.

The red granite stone, forty-four inches high and thirty-six inches wide, is supported by a concrete base forty-four inches long and twenty-four inches wide and stands beside the graves of his parents and grandparents.

The inscription reads:

LYNDON BAINES JOHNSON
AUGUST 27, 1908
JANUARY 22, 1973
36th PRESIDENT
OF THE
UNITED STATES OF AMERICA

A replica of the Presidential Seal is carved below.

Courtesy of Lyndon Baines Johnson Historic Site. Ruth W. Laird Photograph

Lyndon B. Johnson Statue

Courtesy of Lyndon Baines Johnson Historic Site. Ruth W. Laird Photograph

Lyndon B. Johnson and parents and grandparents Grave Monuments in the Johnson Cemetery.

(38)   HUBERT HORATIO HUMPHREY, JR.
January 20, 1965 — January 20, 1969

(Lyndon Baines Johnson — Second Term)

Courtesy of Lakewood Cemetery. Ruth W. Laird Photograph

Hubert H. Humphrey Grave Site.

Hubert Horatio Humphrey, Jr.   Chronology
Thirty-Eighth Vice President
(Lyndon Baines Johnson   Second Term)

1911, May 27	Born at Wallace, South Dakota.
1917	Moves with parents to Doland, South Dakota.
1918	In elementary school, Doland, South Dakota.
1929	Leaves Doland for study at the University of Minnesota.
1932	Attends Capital College of Pharmacy, Denver, Colorado.
1933	Pharmacist, Humphrey Drug Company, Huron, South Dakota.
1936, Sep. 3	Marries Muriel Fay Buck. Father of four children.
1939	AB, University of Minnesota. Elected to Phi Beta Kappa.
1940	MA Degree, University of Louisiana; Assistant Instructor of Political Science.
1941	Graduate Student, University of Minnesota. Administrative Staff W.P.A. Regional Director, War Manpower Commission.
1943	Defeated for Office of Mayor of Minneapolis.
1943–45	Professor of Political Science, Macalester College.
1945	Mayor of Minneapolis. Fails Armed Forces physical.
1946, Dec. 18	Becomes a Master Mason, Cataract Lodge #2, F&AM, Minneapolis, Minnesota. Re-elected Mayor.
1948	Elected U.S. Senator. Advocates health insurance for the elderly.

1954	Re-elected U.S. Senator. LLD, National University Law School.
1960	Re-elected U.S. Senator.
1964	Elected Vice President of the United States. Resigns from the Senate. Pushes Civil Rights Bill through Congress.
1968	Fails to be elected President.
1969	Returns to teaching at Macalester College and University of Minnesota, both in Minneapolis.
1970	Elected United States Senator.
1976	Re-elected United States Senator for fifth term.
1978	Health and Welfare Building dedicated as the Hubert H. Humphrey Building.
1978, Jan. 14	Expires at his home in Minneapolis, Minnesota. Age 66 years.

The burial plot of Vice President Hubert H. Humphrey is located in the Lakewood Cemetery, 3600 Hennepin Avenue, Minneapolis, Minnesota. The plot has a frontage of twenty-five feet and is twenty feet deep.

The rear border is marked by four American flags measuring ten inches by sixteen inches, on poles two feet four inches high.

A nine-foot by twelve-foot chain surrounds the burial site which has a two-foot by one-foot bronze plaque with this inscription:

HUBERT H. HUMPHREY
1911 –1978

Hubert H. Humphrey

Courtesy of Lakewood Cemetery. Ruth W. Laird Photograph

Vice President Hubert H. Humphrey Grave Marker

(39)   SPIRO THEODORE AGNEW
January 20, 1969 — October 10, 1973

(Richard Milhous Nixon — First & Second Terms)

Resigned as Vice President
before the expiration of second term

Spiro Theodore Agnew   Chronology   Thirty-Ninth
                    Vice President
        Nixon   First & Second Terms

1918, Nov. 9	Born at Baltimore, Maryland.
1937	Is graduated from the Forest Park High School.
1937–39	Student at Johns Hopkins University.
1939	Student at Baltimore Law School.
1941	Private in the United States Army.
1942	Is commissioned Second Lieutenant.
1942, June	Marries Judy Judefind. Father of four children.
1945	Earns battlefield promotion to First Lieutenant during Battle of the Bulge.
1946	Released from active duty and admitted to the Maryland Bar.
1947	Receives LLB degree from the Baltimore Law School.
1948	Opens Law office.
1950	Recalled to active duty for the Korean War.
1951	Released from active military duty.
1952	Enrolls in McCoy College.
1953	Joins Kiwanis Club, Loch Raven, MD; 100% attender for seven years.
1958	Appointed to Zoning Appeals Board, Baltimore County.
1962	Defeated in race for the office of Baltimore County Judge.
1966	Elected Governor of Maryland.
1967	Opposes "Open Housing".

1968, April	Activates the Maryland National Guard to quell riots.
1968, Nov.	Elected Vice President of the United States.
1972	Re-elected Vice President.
1973, Oct. 10	Resigns as Vice President.

(40)   GERALD RUDOLPH FORD
December 6, 1973 — August 9, 1974

(Nixon — Second Term)

Was appointed Vice President
by President Nixon October 12, 1973
Succeeded to the Presidency upon
resignation of Nixon, August 9, 1974

Gerald Rudolph Ford   Chronology
        Fortieth Vice President
        (Nixon   Second Term)

1913, July 14	Born at Omaha, Nebraska. Named Leslie Lynch King.
1915	Moves to Grand Rapids, Michigan with his mother.
1919	Adopted by Gerald Rudolph Ford and is named Gerald Rudolph Ford, Jr.
1929	Earns Eagle Scout badge.
1931	Is graduated from South High School, Grand Rapids.
1934	Named All-American Center and receives the Most Valuable Player Trophy at the University of Michigan.
1935	Earns Bachelor of Arts Degree at the University of Michigan. Plays in the East West Shrine football game.
1936	Ranger in the Yellowstone National Park; assistant football coach and boxing coach, Yale University; enrolls in Yale Law School.
1941	Earns LLB Degree, Yale Law School; admitted to the Bar and opens Law office in Grand Rapids, Michigan.
1942	Begins World War II service in the U.S. Navy as Ensign.
1943	Promoted to Lieutenant, Junior Grade and serves under Admiral Halsey as Lieutenant in 1944.
1945	Discharged from active duty with the rank of Lieutenant Commander, USNR and wearing ten battle stars.

1946	Returns to the private practice of Law.
1948, Oct. 15	Marries Elizabeth Bloomer Warren. Father of four children.
	Elected to the House of Representatives.
1950	Re-elected to a second term in Congress.
1951, May 18	Becomes a Master Mason in the Malta Lodge, #465, F&AM Grand Rapids, Michigan.
1954	Refuses to run for the United States Senate.
1962, Sep.	Created Inspector General, Honorary 33d Degree, Ancient Accepted Scottish Rite, Northern Masonic Jurisdiction.
1963	Becomes Honorary Member, DeMolay Legion of Honor.
1964	Elected House of Representatives Minority Leader; serves on Warren Commission to investigate the John F. Kennedy assassination.
1970	Heads movement to impeach a Justice of the United States Supreme Court.
1972	Elected to the thirteenth consecutive term in the United States Congress; visits Communist China.
1973, Oct. 12	Appointed Vice President by President Nixon under the 25th Amendment to the Constitution.
1973, Dec. 6	Sworn in as Vice President of the United States.
1974	Recipient of the Gourgas Medal, the sixteenth medalist of the Supreme Council of the Ancient Accepted Scottish Rite, 33d Degree Northern Masonic Jurisdiction.
1974, Aug. 9	Sworn in as President of the United States upon the resignation of President Richard M. Nixon.
1974, Aug. 20	Appoints Nelson Aldrich Rockefeller to fill the vacancy in the office of Vice President.
1974, Sep. 8	Issues "Blanket Pardon" for former President Nixon.

1975, May	Orders U.S. Marines to liberate captured ship *Mayaguez,* having an American crew. Visits Communist China.
1976	Selects Senator Robert Dole as running mate in Presidential election instead of incumbent Vice President Nelson A. Rockefeller.
1976, Nov. 2	Fails to be elected President.
1977	Takes up residence in Palm Springs, California.
1978	Delivers lectures on political subjects to audiences in colleges and universities.

(41)   NELSON ALDRICH ROCKEFELLER
December 19, 1974 — January 20, 1977
(Ford)

Was appointed Vice President by President Ford,
August 20, 1974

New York Post photograph by Delucia. (C) 1979, New York Post Corporation.

Vice President Nelson A. Rockefeller Grave Marker

Nelson A. Rockefeller   Chronology
Forty-First Vice President
(Ford)

1908, July 8	Born at Bar Harbor, Maine.
1917	Begins preparatory education at the Lincoln School in New York City.
1930	Earns AB Degree at Dartmouth College; elected to Phi Beta Kappa.
1930, June 23	Marries Mary Todhunter Clark. Father of five children.
1932	Appointed to Westchester County Board of Health.
1933	Begins association with Rockefeller business interests.
1937	Tours Latin America.
1940	Coordinator of Office of Inter-American Republic Affairs.
1944	Assistant Secretary of State for Latin American Affairs.
1945	Awarded Order of Merit by Chile. Relieved from State post.
1946	Forms Economic and Social Development Association for South America. Awarded National Order of Southern Cross by Brazil.
1949	Awarded Order of Aztec Eagle by Mexico.
1950	Chairman of International Development Advisory Board.
1953	Appointed Undersecretary of Health, Education and Welfare.
	Chairman of President's Advisory Committee on Government Organization.

344 *Nelson Aldrich Rockefeller*

1955	Special assistant to the President. Awarded Gold Medal by National Planning Association.
1956	Chairman of Commission on the Constitutional Convention of New York. President of Rockefeller Bros. Fund.
1958	Elected to first term as Governor of New York.
1959	Begins expansion of State University System from 28 campuses to 71. Receives Ramon Magsaysay Award from the Philippines.
1961	Receives Universal Brotherhood Medal from the Jewish Theological Seminary. Separates from first wife.
	Launches plans for Albany Mall.
1962	Author of *The Future of Federalism*. Obtains divorce.
	Re-elected Governor of New York.
1963, May 4	Marries Margaretta Fitler Murphy. Father of two children.
1964	Fails in bid to be nominated as Republican Presidential candidate.
1965	Recipient of the Charles Evans Hughes Medal from the National Conference of Christians and Jews.
1967	Awarded Gold Medal by the National Institute of Social Sciences. Begins third term as Governor of New York.
1968	Author of *Unity, Freedom and Peace*.
1970	Author of *Our Environment Can Be Saved*. Receives Conservation and Water Management Award from Great Lakes Commission. Elected to fourth term as Governor of New York.
1971, Sep.	Refuses to interfere in settling Attica Prison riot.

1973	Dedicates Albany Mall as "the most beautiful government buildings in the world."
1973, Dec.	Resigns as Governor of New York to devote time to water quality and preserving the environment.
1974, Aug. 20	Nominated by President Ford to fill the office of Vice President of the United States.
1974, Dec. 19	Sworn in as Vice President of the United States.
1975	$100 billion plan to solve energy crisis rejected.
1975	First Vice President to occupy the Official Residence of the Vice President of the United States.
1976	Not selected by Gerald R. Ford to be his running mate in the November election.
1977	Announces his retirement from politics. Becomes an Art Aficionado.
1978	Plans to publish books on his art collection. Opens store to sell reproductions from his collection.
1979, Jan. 26	Passes away in his townhouse in New York City at the age of 70 years.*
1979, Feb. 2	Memorial service held in Riverside Church, Upper Manhattan attended by President Jimmy Carter and Vice President Walter Mondale and other public figures. The Principal eulogy delivered by former Secretary of State, Henry Kissinger.

*The first Vice President of the United States to have his remains cremated.

The monument marking the grave of Vice President Nelson A. Rockefeller is located in the private burial plot on his estate at Pocantico Hills, North Tarrytown, New York. It is a marble slab eighteen inches wide and twenty-four inches high carrying this inscription:

NELSON
ALDRICH
ROCKEFELLER

BORN + BAR HARBOR
MAINE
JULY 8th 1908
DIED + NEW YORK
NEW YORK
JANUARY 26th 1979

(42)　　WALTER FREDERICK MONDALE
January 20, 1977 —

(Carter)

Ruth W. Laird Photograph

Official residence of the United States Vice President. Nelson A. Rockefeller was the first Vice President to occupy the mansion in 1975.

Walter Frederick Mondale   Chronology
Forty-Second Vice President
(Carter)

1928, Jan. 5	Born at Ceylon, Minnesota.
1951	Earns Bachelor of Arts Degree, Cum Laude, University of Minnesota.
1951–53	Serves in the Army of the United States in the Korean Conflict.
1955, Dec. 27	Marries Joan Adams. Father of three children.
1956	Earns LLB Degree, University of Minnesota Law School.
1960	Attorney General of Minnesota. Named Outstanding Young Man of the Year of Minnesota.
1964	United States Senator, first of two terms.
1976	Elected Vice President.
1977, Jan. 20	Vice President of the United States.

INDEX

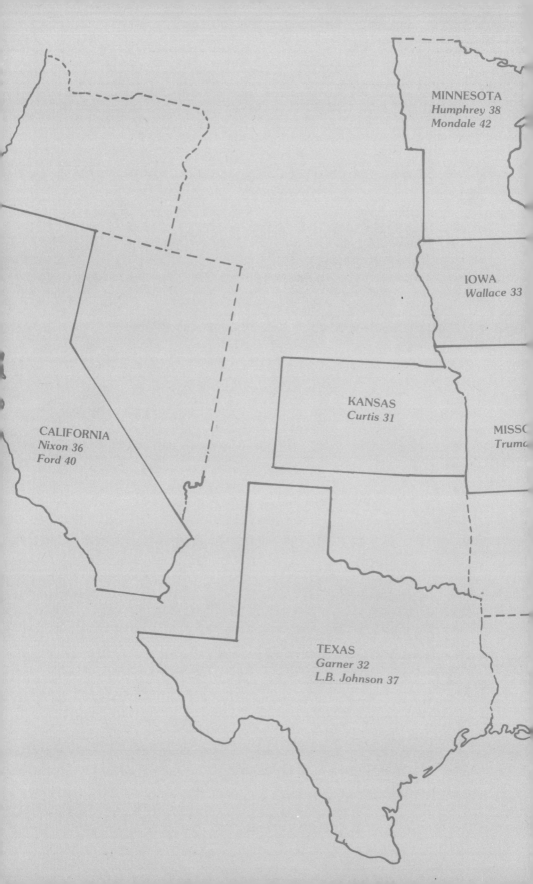

MINNESOTA
Humphrey 38
Mondale 42

IOWA
Wallace 33

KANSAS
Curtis 31

MISSO
Trum

CALIFORNIA
Nixon 36
Ford 40

TEXAS
Garner 32
L.B. Johnson 37